PART ONE

Blood-Soaked Soil

My Story

From Early Life in Communist Yugoslavia
to the First Months of War

Mario Bekes

First published by Busybird Publishing 2021

Copyright © 2021 Mario Bekes

978-1-922465-93-1 (paperback)
978-1-922465-94-8 (ebook)

This work is copyright. Apart from any use permitted under the *Copyright Act 1968*, no part of this publication may be reproduced, stored in a retrieval system or transmitted in any form or by any means, electronic, mechanical, photocopying, recording or otherwise, without the prior written permission of Mario Bekes.

Cover Image: Busybird Publishing, Pixabay

Cover design: Busybird Publishing

Layout and typesetting: Busybird Publishing

Busybird Publishing
2/118 Para Road
Montmorency, Victoria
Australia 3094
www.busybird.com.au

*This book is dedicated to my son Matteo Gaetano,
who has become a better man than I could ever possibly dream.*

*You, my son, you are the one who inspired me, schooled me
and provided me with energy from the moment you were born.*

About the Author

Mario Bekes was born in Croatia in 1972, then part of the communist country of Yugoslavia. After an unhappy childhood, he found himself in the centre of the Croatian War of Independence in the 1990s. He was eighteen.

Mario went on to witness some of the most distressing scenes imaginable and spent 1,852 consecutive days in combat, risking his life on a daily basis.

He commenced his career serving in the Ministry of Interior (Special Forces), then transitioning to Ministry of Defence (Military Police and Security Services) for seven years before working in diplomatic security intelligence (Directorate 7) for the Croatian Government. In 1998 he joined the Department of Foreign Affairs in Security Intelligence Services, with a secondment to the Consulate General in Sydney for a further five years.

During his extensive military and diplomatic career Mario completed numerous courses – some of them in urban warfare, counter-terrorism, intelligence security protection and other related fields in investigations and intelligence operations.

Mario is proficient in three languages (English, Croatian and Russian). He has written several books and articles on investigations, human intelligence and information risk management, as well as hosting a business radio show on Alive 90.5 FM.

Mario has conducted numerous internal and external investigation in corporate, government sectors in Australia and overseas, particularly in the field of human intelligence and competitive business intelligence.

Mario now runs a successful investigation and information risk company, Insight Intelligence Group, which he founded in 2003. He cites his son's health battles as a source of inspiration. He is also an ambassador of the Shining Light Foundation, caring for the homeless in Sydney, Australia.

Content

Foreword	1
The Boy Who Just Wanted Love and a Hug	3
Croatia: A Country Kept Apart	7
You Don't Choose Your Parents	11
Not a Christmas to Wish For	15
First Love	21
The Moment the Magic Stopped	25
World Falling Apart	29
Boy to Adult, Dreamer to Soldier	33
Blood-Soaked Soil	39
The Ten Commandments	43
Training	45
The Summer of 1991	49
Kill the Fear or Die	53
The Village	59
'Mum' – The Last Word Every Man Says	65
Village of the Damned	67
Grandparents and Insulin	81
No Candles on My Birthday Cake	87
Kids are Safe, But Parents are Hanging in the Closet	93
Surrounded	97
Let Me Sleep, Please	101
Curing the Pneumonia with Grappa	105
The Cornfields	109
The Water Pump	117
Fallen, Broken, Jesus	123
The University	127
The End of the War	135
Afterword	139
Index	143

Foreword

Nick Hill

I first met Mario Bekes in 2014 when he and I worked together on a study looking at the personal information that businesses discard through their recycle bins and second-hand hard drives. As a seasoned marketing professional, I was helping to communicate the risks to the public, and Mario's team had done the investigative work collating the data.

Mario brings the biggest positive energy into a room out of anyone I have ever met. Since then, we have worked together on a number of different projects, and I have learnt even more about the man through helping him to tell his incredible story. It has been a fascinating experience.

A few months prior to meeting Mario, I visited the stunningly beautiful city of Dubrovnik in Croatia and learnt a little about its recent wartime history. What struck me most was that I was at university when the battles took place and I remember watching them on the news. Until then, I had never considered that, had I lived in Croatia in another life, I would have been heavily involved in the horrors of war rather than sitting in a cosy UK lecture hall.

Reading this book, it is hard to imagine the hardships faced by people in Croatia and across former Yugoslavia during the conflicts, let alone the intensity of Mario's personal experiences.

We are lucky to have Mario here to tell his story and inspire us with the knowledge that, despite being involved in situations you would not wish on anyone, a person can come out with a positive attitude and seek to brighten people's days.

I challenge everyone to read this book and imagine themselves as an 18-year-old, suddenly finding their world has turned on its head, with a hostile tank hurtling down the road towards you – with its self-confident captain crunching an apple! The mental scars will always run deep, but it is how you respond that defines you.

Mario, thank you for writing this book and being a shining beacon for everyone around you. I look forward to the next instalment and its further insight into your amazing life experiences.

The Boy Who Just Wanted Love and a Hug

"I was that boy – the boy who, from the age of five, was being told, 'you are nothing, you will be nothing and no one cares for you'."

Welcome to the world of Mario Bekes. This is a true story.

My story is based on true events and I want to share this story with you in a simple way. English is not my first language – in fact, my English language skills are a disaster (even with a little help from my friends).

I am pretty sure you'll believe you have heard stories like mine. I contend you have not, however, for one simple reason – this is *my* life. These events happened to me, and my thoughts and emotions are still very raw.

The following events and accounts begin on the day I was born and continue until 1992. You could say it's a mixture of the blockbuster movies: *Saving Private Ryan*, Jason Bourne and *The Girl with the Dragon Tattoo*.

I was born in 1972, the Year of the Rat. My story involves a lot of pain, and not understanding as a child why I could not be loved. I was the boy who wandered into the arms of those who would give me some attention. Unfortunately, I was always on wrong side of the law, outcast by society and my parents. Not having friends and the choices I made as a child is what defines me today.

I was born into one of the most fucked up countries on the planet, which appeared strong on paper and existed almost five decades before disintegrating in just a few months. With it went all the beliefs that had been drilled into us as young children.

Imagine being born into a society that does not allow you to think, talk freely or even desire some new Nike sneakers. The society I grew up in was communist – based on hard-core discipline and being on constant alert from external enemies, while internal enemies were dealt by the Secret Police and state security services.

As a child, there was a sense of unease of living under Yugoslavian communist control. I witnessed the majority of my fellow countrymen wanting Croatia to become an independent country. However, there were many ethnic Serbs living there who were opposed to this. With support from Serbia, they started trying to claim our land for themselves to create a new Serbian State that included areas of Croatia and Bosnia and Herzegovina. This culminated in the Croatian War of Independence.

This story does not involve a princess, a knight on the white horse, nor does it involve dwarves and unicorns. This is a story about growing up with parents who do not want you, about making the wrong choices and hanging out with wrong crowd.

I was a thug and thief. I was a terrible student in school, the worst of the worst. I could not complete my homework. I spent less time studying and more time on the street. Almost all my grades were barely a pass. I was the type of a student parents told their kids, "Don't associate yourself with that Mario Bekes." It is true. I was that boy – the boy who was told from the age of five,

'You are nothing, you will be nothing and no one cares for you.'

I have been through juvenile detention and military school, and experienced the horrors of war. I have witnessed sheer destruction, death, suffering and broken hearts.

Throughout my childhood, I did things I do not want anyone to do. I was stealing from shops and from friends, and fighting older guys because I was bullied for being fat, round and stupid. I knew I needed to make my name on the streets, so I went to a local boxing club, which was basically only for 'bad boys'. I was never built for football – imagine me, playing striker! Instead, I learnt how to fight. Boxing was my choice.

I met guys who were in the prison system. One day at a music concert I was told to stab a guy with a screwdriver because he was looking at some girl. So, what did I do? At age thirteen, I took the screwdriver and stabbed the guy twice, was arrested and placed in in a juvenile detention centre. I deserved it.

I was lucky that my grandfather worked his magic and I was able to leave after a few weeks. He was a high ranking communist police officer, a general. He was a moral, ethical, righteous man, and he truly believed in justice. He was a Croatian and believed in an independent Croatia – even though nationalism was forbidden in Yugoslavia. This belief eventually cost him. He was then considered to be spying for the enemy, which was not true.

This story is all about dreaming, imagining and hoping. It's the story of the boy who dreamed about only one thing: love, and to be loved: by parents, by friends… by a woman. Is this a love story? Yes, it is a love story – but it's not a love story where the princess is in the castle waiting for her prince. Oh, there is a woman – and that woman has forever marked my existence. She gave me a purpose for my future.

In one simple stroke of the pen, we became enemies, simply because we belonged to different nationalities. We were separated by 100 km of pure hate, anger, vengeance and the desire to destroy each other. I was eighteen years old and I wanted to die – not because I was not loved, but because I could not be with the one I loved.

This story may be full of uncertainty, full of horror stories and unhappiness – but in spite of that, there is always something there, something you should always believe exists – and that is hope. Trust me. One thing I can prove is that miracles *do* exist. All the tools you need to be happy, successful and loved are inside you, inside all of us.

Perhaps after reading my story you will see that you don't need gurus, podcasters and life or business coaches. You can be one yourself.

Croatia: A Country Kept Apart

"Croatia is a beautiful country. If you can imagine the most beautiful country, it is Croatia."

This story begins on the day I was born. That was far, far away and a long time ago – on the 17th September in 1972, in Yugoslavia and the Socialist Republic of Croatia.

I was born in a place called Osijek. The city is in the East of Croatia, in an intersection between the borders of Hungary and Serbia. Throughout the century, it was a battleground between the East and the West – Romans versus Eastern tribes, and the Austrian-Hungarian monarchy versus the Ottoman Empire.

Croatia is a beautiful country. If you can imagine the most beautiful country, it is Croatia. You must visit this place. Surrounded by an endless sea that is calm and inviting, it's also home to mountains wrapped in pristine beauty, rivers and national parks, and green fields of corn, sunflowers, wheat and barley. A word of friendly warning, though – prepare yourself if you ever come to visit. You will likely be ripped off. The people love to take advantage of tourists, but if you visit family or relatives it's a different story. You will be killed with love by how much they look after you.

I remember Osijek from very early age. It was a beautiful city, surrounded in endless fields, all green. I remember riding on the tram, along its circle from East to West. It connected one part of the city to the other. It was built a long, long time ago during the reign of the Austrian-Hungarian monarchy. Today the track has been expanded in all directions. I can still remember seeing people on the tram going to work.

The city I knew as a child was surrounded by natural beauty and amazing architecture. This was the kind of city you mostly see in Switzerland, small with everything you need. That city ceased to exist in the summer of 1991 due to heavy shelling and the destruction of war.

I was born in Yugoslavia and my city was a part of the Socialist Republic of Croatia. It was a typical communist country – a little more advanced than the Eastern Block, but still a communist country. Yugoslavia consisted of six republics and two territories, all amalgamated into the one country. It had a communist ideology, socialist lifestyle and, most importantly, a forbidden love with the West, the Church and democracy.

Communism was a 'safe' society, with no weapons and almost no criminals. You could walk the streets at 3am with no fear. It was a peaceful environment to live in.

From early age, you were being continuously pumped up with the beliefs of the generation before you, who had fought for independence – how the freedom fighters had fought against the capitalists and everything else.

We were told Yugoslavia had the best lifestyle and freedoms, which was an utter lie. If you wanted to go to another republic, you would not understand their language. You would not understand their writing. It was a combustible mixture of different nations, controlled by the state Secret Police. Nationalism and patriotism were not allowed.

Everything was being oriented in that way to cherish how you lived. Local writers and music were good, while everything outside was bad. Anything outside, such as rock and roll, was seen as a bad influence, and this would be further reinforced by TV documentaries.

If something was forbidden, you could be arrested. It was forbidden to listen to foreign news. I remember my father would go into the bathroom every morning with a small radio and listen to *The Voice of America*. He would listen under a blanket in the bathtub secretly and discreetly so that not even the neighbours could hear him. He told me that if I said anything, he would kill me.

You would hear every day about the heroes of the communist revolution – Stalin, Lenin, Marx and Engels. They were all compulsory parts of our education.

I was taught how to use a rifle from the age of ten. I had a carbine M-48 calibre 7.9mm. They place it in your hands, and you were being educated on how to defend your country. As kids living under communism rule, we believed we were invincible. Once you had an understanding of democracy, you found this to be a very weak society.

Communism was an ideology, and socialism was the way of living. As kids we believed in the system. When you're born into this environment, you believe you're descendants from the Gods. *False.* This changed as we grew up, and as adults we began fearing speaking out against the regime. The kids would report this to appropriate channels.

Throughout history, Croatia was always on the side of the Germans, Austrians and Italians. The Second World War marked Croatia as a country who committed atrocities towards other nationalities like the Jews and gypsies, all driven by the idea of 'purity'.

You cannot choose where you are born, though. You cannot choose who your parents are. You cannot choose what school you are going to. This is something given to all of us at birth. It is a given, but you can make your choices a little later.

I was lucky enough to be born in 1972 for one simple reason. Life has allowed me to better understand things when I see them from today's perspective – seeing what life was like in communism and then in democracy, with the difference in technologies and the evolution of society.

You Don't Choose Your Parents

"I only remember my father belting me, bashing me, breaking things on me."

My parents were interesting characters. My father was born in 1936, and my mother in 1952. Sixteen years is a big age difference. But that was my father – he loved the younger girls. My father's parents were peasants, so you could say he didn't know any better.

Somehow, he ended up in Germany. He was a welder and he adored German discipline and accuracy. Again, I have no idea why he came back or what he earned – zero information whatsoever.

I have no idea how my parents met either. To be honest, I don't know how they even contemplated being together in the first place. I would like to say something more about my parents – however, their entire story is murky because it was always hidden and never spoken in front of me. When I look back at my childhood, there were a million unknown things about my parents. Do I blame them for not sharing more with me? Most probably. Perhaps if I had known more, I could have understood what was happening in their heads and why they were behaving in a certain way.

I was an unwanted child, born into a family I never understood. I only had one sibling. My parents chose to love my brother, yet displayed nothing but loathing, anger and rage towards me. There was no feeling the love from my parents.

Imagine a two-bedroom apartment with all four of us inside. I remember my father would wake up at 4:30 in the morning and start work at 6am. He would wake up, make himself a black Turkish coffee and sit down at a table, day after day, night after night.

The apartment stank from cigarette smoke from early morning. Then my mum would rise around 5am after my dad had made coffee and woken her up. They had their coffee together, scheming together. They both worked in the same factory, called Kandit. They made sugar, candies and chocolates. Nothing involved me and I was not concerned.

We never had a car. My father could walk to work in fifteen minutes and would get around by bike. I never understood why my parents could not get a car. Later, I discovered a car was luxury for them, while five packets of smokes per day were not.

My father was of fragile build, very short with his big ears and big nose, like a little mouse. He was afraid of his own shadow, and the only way he would express emotion was by punishing me. He was brutal. I do not remember any loving behaviour. I only remember my father belting me, bashing me, breaking things on me and breaking my bed frame. He would come to my bed at 2 o'clock in the morning and punch me in the face for no reason. I was just a kid. I was five or six years old.

It was quite typical for parents in communism to smash, kick and slap their kids, but my father took it to another level. It was not just the way he would walk into my room to punch me in the face just because he could. Some of the things he did to me bordered on insanity. He was a man with a sheer dedication to destroying and torturing me day after day. I think he deserved the Oscar for creativity in brutality and sadism. I can laugh about it today because I know that kids can be raised without that kind of brutality. I could have turned out like my father, but I did not.

In 1979, I got my first bike. However, before I got the bike, my father belted me so hard that I bled, just to remind me how much he'd sacrificed to get me the bike.

All that he loved was a beer, a coffee and my mum. He also had a big mouth, and was always going on about what we should be doing and that we should kill this and that.

Every day would consist of my mother bashing me in the morning and then my father bashing me after work and at night. There was no need for my parents to punch me in the face or to belt me. No, they just did it because they could.

I learned that my mum, despite being born in a good family, had gone into hairdressing as her father was trying to hide her in this kind of job. She was a compulsive liar and a kleptomaniac, stealing from people and their homes. That was her way of life.

In communist Yugoslavia, school and education is free. You could have as much as sick leave as you wanted so long as you could provide a medical certificate. It was a traditional model, with mothers always looking after the children.

My mum was always taking sick leave. Despite this, if I was sick, she would send me to school, while she would stay home for three months. That was my mum. She got paid and I got sent to school. If she ever did have to look after me, she would play the victim as it meant she could not work.

When you were born with parents like mine, you look at other parents and feel sad that you were an unwanted kid. I realised from an early age that my parents would rather spend money on all the smokes and alcohol that their money could buy. They would never keep promises and you would never have better sneakers, new trousers or a new school bag. Nothing, nothing.

All I had was a dream. As a child I always dreamt one day I'd have a better life, starting with better sneakers! A pair of Nikes was more like science fiction than a dream for me. When I was growing up only a very lucky few had been able to get hold of things like Nike or Adidas sneakers, or Fila and Reebok tracksuits.

In September and October, my parents would buy hundreds of kilos of potato, capsicum and tomatoes that my mum would make into sauces. Then in November, they would eventually kill the biggest pig on the planet, then prepare the meat. We would have small bits of meat so it would last us until April or May, always accompanied by the freshest juice we could buy.

I could not imagine asking my father to buy fresh meat in the shops – he would destroy me. Anyway, in the late 70s and 80s there were big restrictions on things like petrol, coffee, cooking oil and sugar etc. I used to stand in front of the shops for eight, nine, ten hours at a time, just waiting in line so my mum could come and trade places with me.

It was a bad time – there were shortages of everything. It is hard to imagine now – waiting in line for hours, just to get essentials. We did not know anything different. Communism was bad, but we could not rebel or speak out about our unhappiness.

The first six years of my life were very tragic. However, what came next was even worse.

Not a Christmas to Wish For

"What kind of human kicks their child out on a cold Christmas Eve – just because you can?"

In Croatia, churches were common, but they were also very empty places. Church doors were open and, mostly, you'd only see very old people in there. Hardly any middle age or younger people would go.

I didn't know what the church was. I was born into a very poor family. They didn't have faith in anything, except total negativity. My father hated everybody. He was always envious and jealous. Imagine, every morning you wake up, instead of having your parents wish you a good morning, they say, "Today's going to be a terrible day."

We never practiced any religious holidays like Christmas or Easter. I do remember one thing about Christmas and Easter growing up – they were always very sad days. Instead of celebrating, my parents would fight constantly and be drunk from the early morning.

I used to watch the kids in my street at Christmas and Easter. They'd get some presents and be rewarded somehow by their parents, cousins and siblings. I don't remember seeing many people going into church or practicing faith.

As a child, there were two men who changed my life. One was my grandfather, who gave me some support. He did not know how to say he loved me, but I knew he did. He would hug me and give me money to buy food. He would tell me in a nice way, "Don't do these things. Do not rob people. Do not steal. Do not lie." He never directly said, *"Do not be like my daughter."*

My grandfather didn't go to church, but he did believe in God. I'm pretty sure he would pray, but being a high ranking party member and part of the Secret Communist Police, he was not allowed to go into church. If he had, it would have been used against him in some shape or form.

The second man was a priest called Matej. I became an altar boy, almost by chance. I was a born Roman Catholic and baptised, but it was really just an excuse for my parents to drink and celebrate. They never practiced the faith and never went to church or masses.

Once, when I was a young boy, only five or six years old, I ran into the church to hide from being bullied, being calling fatso, being ridiculed by the older boys. I was just a kid, and I was alone. My knees and elbows were bleeding and I was covered in scratches.

There was a nice nun at the door. She asked me, "Son, what are you doing?" I was very afraid, I'd never seen a nun in my life. I told her some lie.

She told me to come inside and watch a movie, so I went inside. There was a strong smell of incense, but it was incredibly clean. It was a movie about Jesus. There was a big old projector and a few other kids there in the dark. I began falling in love with the idea of going to church.

I became the altar boy and the priest, Matej, was a very nice man. He was a good priest, and he trusted me. I thought this was an awesome place. Somebody was showing me that I do not need to be afraid of expressing myself, and that there are the people who love me. They knew I was lost in a kind of space. The beautiful thing was that Matej was showing me the way like my grandfather had, without ever telling me 'I love you'.

It gave me the confidence to do things. I would collect the money, run the Mass, take responsibility and have accountability. I really loved it. I remember every word the priest said at Mass. I really liked everything that happened at church. It was very peaceful and I loved the flowers. Everybody was nice to me, even when I was naughty.

Other kids did not know that I was going into church. I would certainly have been made fun of and called a liar. Many kids did not go to church anyway, as their parents were members of the Communist Party.

One day Matej told my dad that I was good boy and all I needed was a little love. My father did not know what to say – but he did know what to do when the priest left. He bashed me.

It was coming up to Christmas 1986. I was fourteen years old. Every year the factory my parents worked in organised a Christmas event for the children, giving gifts with sweets, candles, books and toys. My parents did not tell me about this.

That evening, by pure chance I remember I was walking around the suburb and went inside the factory. I saw the kids getting presents. I wanted a present and knew I should get one, so I walked up onto the stage, following the other children. I remember people whispering, and I could imagine that my name was not on list, but some gentleman told me to sit in Santa's lap. They took a picture as well.

Needless to say, the following day my father found all of this out and broke a chair on me. Then my mother came back from work that evening, took the biggest wooden spoon which they used to cook jam, and broke it on my knee.

That was just a few days before Christmas. I was in such pain, I just wanted to die. I just wanted to run away. I remember it was snowing a lot. It was white outside and there were no mobile phones, no Twitter, no Facebook, nothing. I had nobody to call, nobody to talk to. I was just staring through the window, watching the snow. My nose was bleeding and my knee was broken. I did not dare ask anything else. I had fought to save my gift from Santa Claus and my father just threw it in the garbage.

This is how my dream was being killed. At that point, I did not have any anger. I did not have any feelings at all, except sadness and being in pain.

A few days later it was Christmas Eve. I came home from school and was waiting for my mum to make me dinner. My parents were looking at each other. I just felt that something was wrong.

My father took my school bag and pulled out the few things I had it in. He grabbed me by the throat, lifting me clean off the floor. He threw me out down the stairs and told me not to come back home ever again.

It was very cold. People were coming from the shops. They were buying last-minute things for Christmas and I was standing in that mall on my own.

I think my teeth were frozen, or at least that is the best way I can describe it. I had been kicked out in just a t-shirt and track pants. I was standing in the snow with my school bag and a few of my things inside. Everybody was avoiding me, like I had the plague. It was really hard to comprehend all of this.

My grandfather appeared, well dressed like a man of stature. He wiped the blood off my face, took his coat off to give to me, then took me to his home.

I still remember the way my grandfather's wife, Rose, just looked at me. She gave me food and washed me. She told me, "You are going to sleep here, and tomorrow morning we will do something else."

What kind of people were my parents? What kind of human kicks their child out on a cold Christmas Eve – just because you can? At least I knew that my grandfather loved me and was going to do everything he could to protect me.

The following day, this man who loved me, who'd imparted his values and beliefs to me, told me the plan to send me away to school where I would learn skills, be respected by society and most importantly become independent from my parents.

First Love

Everybody dreams about love. I never had a girlfriend or kissed a girl until I was eighteen. Growing up, I'd sit with my friends and exchange stories. I know some boys were 'luckier' than others. I think I was the most unfortunate one – but I enjoyed my friends' stories of how they were having sex, how they kissed the girls.

Of course I lied about how many girls I had been with, and I was laughed at. Everyone would look at me like, "You?"

I'd say, "Yeah, of course, you know what I mean..." Lie after lie.

My imagination never ended. The reality was that I was looking to have the girl who everybody wanted – the best in the class, best in the school, best in the street and the best looking. Now let me tell you, each time I met a girl like this, I would fall in love. I was falling in love left, right and centre. But none of the girls ever noticed me.

It did not help that their mothers used to be saying to girls in my school, "Do not associate yourself with that Mario. He is a thug, he's a thief, he's a criminal." All these names would kill any desire to be with me.

I was always the third wheel – or, in reality, more of a twelfth or sixteenth wheel! I was doing anything and everything just to be noticed – but I was never noticed, unless it was for my stupid behaviour.

Then, just by chance, I met a girl in Zagreb, the capital city of Croatia. It was the autumn of 1990 and I had just turned eighteen. I remember I was so happy when I saw her face for the very first time. I didn't know she was going to be the love of my life, my first sexual encounter, or anything. I just knew I wanted to be with her.

She was fifteen years old. I was three years older and finishing high school. She was so innocent, with big brown eyes and short, brown hair. She had all these freckles on her face and she was so cute. I did not even know how to attract a girl. I think, in my defence, I was a bit older than her and that helped. I like to believe I was The One for her.

We started dating. We would walk around the streets of Zagreb every afternoon and every evening. I loved those moments with her. Whenever I was going back to my home city, went on holiday or was sick, I knew I could not wait to see her. In those times there were no mobile phones or instant communication.

I didn't hide my happiness. I made sure everyone knew. I remember asking her for a picture of her and she said she needed me to take a picture first. When she gave me the picture, she wrote on the back, *'Love me tender, love me true'*.

I carried this picture with me everywhere for years. I had her picture on my wall. I wanted everybody to see. I carried it in my pocket and my happiness was endless. I truly believed I was invincible and that our love was going to last forever. We were inseparable, and could not live without each other. I knew that this was real love. For the very first time I felt that somebody wanted me for who I was and what I was. This was going to be the most beautiful love story ever.

We became more and more intimate. The kissing progressed. I was the first man she'd ever had sex with, and she was the first girl

I'd had sex with. Things were very special between us, and we even discussed how many kids we were going to have together.

Then, just like that, we went to one of the big protests in the capital city, where Croatia was declaring independence. We saw that things were changing so rapidly. The mood of the people was becoming very volatile. The desire for independence creates emotions in people that are hard to understand.

When I was eighteen, I didn't know what independence was. I was part of Yugoslavia, living in Croatia. I was supposed to be an officer of the Yugoslav People's Army. I didn't know anything, but I did see nationalism was expanding. Radicalism was on the corner of every street. Suddenly, newspapers started carrying stories about Croatian independence.

We were like two innocent bystanders, like in the movies. We didn't know what was happening. I didn't realise that, although she was in Croatia, she was a Serbian national. I was Croatian.

We didn't pay much attention to the fact that Yugoslavia was falling apart around us, along with the explosion of Croatian nationalism and call to arms to fight for independence. We simply held each other's hands, gazing into one another's eyes. We had just had sex for the first time and the desire to be together was strong. I didn't want to let her go.

In the spring of 1991, the nationalism reached new levels and I knew our relationship was going to end. There were going to be no fireworks and happiness, just that we were going to both suffer. I'd gone from expecting us to end up living together, to her being 120km away. The only way I could reach her was to call her uncle's phone – just to hear her voice.

I didn't have a car, but we made plans to see each other. I was going to visit her and I knew her parents were aware of my existence. It was an age when you couldn't hide the fact you were seeing someone from your parents – and in communism, everybody knew where you were, what you were doing and who you saw, regardless of where you were or how far away you travelled. Everybody knew something.

The end of the school year arrived. I remember we held hands and said, "Okay, school is finished, see you next Saturday." I travelled to her city, just to spend the afternoon in a park kissing her. Everything was green, there was the smell of freshly cut grass and we would just sit on a bench like two idiots, oblivious to the events around us. After a few hours, I was back on the train to my city.

Our love rapidly became a forbidden love. We didn't know what was happening around us, only that the life we knew had ceased to exist.

The Moment the Magic Stopped

"We knew that somehow our love was becoming forbidden, and for one simple reason: she was Serbian, and I was Croatian."

Our world was coming to an end. Suddenly, there were barricades across Croatia. Religion was dividing and separating cities from the suburbs. The mood amongst the people became very tense. It was Serbs versus Croatians, and Croatian independents versus the rest of Yugoslavia.

I felt like I was going to die if I didn't see her. We kept talking to each other through letters. We wrote on a daily basis, often several letters a day. We knew that somehow our love was becoming forbidden, and for one simple reason: she was Serbian, and I was Croatian.

Her parents did everything they could do to slow down our communication. Suddenly, I couldn't reach her on the phone at her uncle's place.

I remember speaking to my parents about the future. My father was a big nationalist. He knew we needed to stand up and defend democracy. We needed independence. Nothing else was important to him.

One afternoon I picked up the phone and called her uncle. He told me, "Wait, and call again in thirty minutes." So I did, and when she answered the phone, I just felt the summer had become brighter and warmer.

I asked, "What's happening? Please, tell me, what's going on? I haven't been able to reach you for days. You don't reply to my letters anymore." Normally her replies had been arriving in just two days. She started crying, and told me she was going to leave her home in a few hours.

I hung up and phoned my friend, who was a bit older than me. "Can you drive me?" I asked.

We drove like maniacs in some old car. I thought the car was going to explode it was so old, it was falling apart.

I stepped up to her front door and her stepfather came down. He stood tall and looked me straight in the eye, saying, "She is not for you. You are Croatian, and you deserve to die."

I waited in front of the house. They were packing the car. They were leaving.

We followed them as they left. For some brief moment I remember thinking, "This is going to be our love story. It is just a temporary setback."

I could see her in the car, looking out through the back window. I was in the car behind her. Then they crossed the border into Bosnia.

"I have no petrol anymore," my friend told me. "I need to stop now."

The last thing I saw was her crying in the car window as they crossed the bridge over the river.

My friend told me, "Don't cry. You know, everything's going to be okay."

Deep down I knew nothing was going to be okay after this.

I came back to my city that evening. My parents were drunk as usual.

My mother asked, "What is it?" and I explained it to her.

"You are idiot, you are moron," she told me. "What do you know about love? You don't know about life," and I just said to her, "I just love her. I love being with her, I'm happy." My mum just laughed at me.

My father added, "You're not for each other. She's a Serbian, you're a Croatian."

I would say to myself, *"Is this like a Romeo and Juliet story? Is it?"*

With everybody telling me she was not for me, I needed to change somehow and say, *'I can't love her anymore.'* That was on the 3rd July, 1991, after 8pm.

World Falling Apart

"They told me I was scheduled to report to the army barracks immediately. I told them I'd just woken up."

That night, I drank. I drank with my friends and I don't remember what time I came home.

There was always a glimpse of hope inside that things would go back to normal, that it was just temporary or a bad dream. You want to wake up, so you keep pouring more and more alcohol down your throat in the hope that it will change things.

I noticed something else that night. It was summer and in my city we had a recreation centre called Copacabana. Every year the swimming pools played host to the 'Summer of the Youth' event, with local bands form across Yugoslavia playing. But this year there was no music, and the pools were empty. People must have been just sitting at home.

Something big was definitely happening. Moreover, I realised that some of my friends were missing – my Croatian and Serbian friends. When I asked people where they were, I would just get blank stares and, "I don't know. I don't know what's happening or why we are not meeting each other anymore."

The night started with drinking and ended with drinking. I came home – I was drunk and a very, very sad person. My heart was breaking into a million pieces. I just wanted to wake up in the morning and for everything to just go back to normal.

The following morning was 14 July 1991, and I woke to a hard knocking on my door. I knew something was happening, but I didn't know what. I knew I had been drunk and must have been in some fight, judging by the bruises on my face and blood on my knuckles. The knocking on the door was so vigorous, so aggressive, I didn't know what to think.

I was hoping my mum or my dad would open the door, but nobody did. I could smell the alcohol on my breath, and I opened the door. Standing there were four police officers, with two military policemen and two of the regular police.

Let me explain something about the police at that time. The regular civilian police, called militia, wore official uniforms with a red star on their hats. They were easily recognisable across the whole of Yugoslavia. Croatians had started arming themselves in the 1990s and now there was a new breed of military police – the Croatian Police.

The officers give me some papers and told me I was scheduled to report to the army barracks immediately. I told them I'd just woken up.

One of the regular police officers explained to the military officers that they should go and get the others first, then come back for me. "Yes, of course," I said.

The officer said I might want to go to the army barracks by myself. I didn't really understand what was happening. I said I would go to the barracks in the next few hours.

I slowly closed the door and looked around. I couldn't see my mum, my father or my brother. It is not a big unit, just fifty-six square metres, so it wasn't like it was a maze or anything.

I walked slowly through the unit, finding everything was in perfect order, except the balcony door had been shut. We always had the door open in summer. Then I noticed a small piece of white paper on the kitchen table. As I moved towards the table, out the window I saw lots of cars being packed with suitcases and pieces of furniture. I noticed some of them were my friends and it struck me that they were Serbian, Orthodox. Standing there, looking out the window, an uncontrollable shiver went through me. Everything was happening so quickly.

Still wearing just my undies, I sat at the table and read the note. It simply said, "We are okay. Goodbye."

I tried to grasp the reality of what was actually happening, but I couldn't. My father betrayed me. He left me, his child, to stay in a war, while he disappeared. He left me on my own and went off with his wife and younger son.

I made a coffee – no fancy coffee machines from George Clooney, just pure Turkish coffee – boil the water and put coffee inside.

I watched people I'd known for eighteen years leaving their homes, the same people who used to dob me in to my parents about how bad I was. I took that piece of paper, my coffee, a smoke and sat on the balcony. It was 9am. I said, *fuck*, something bad is happening. I started crying and sat there for a full fifteen minutes before going and dressing myself.

At the bottom of my building was a coffee shop. In there were all the tough guys I used to envy and be afraid of. They asked me, "Mario, where the fuck you going?", and I told them I was going to the army barracks. Where else was I to go? I had the military police on my back and I needed to report to the unit.

In that moment, I realised it was the end of my life as I knew it.

I was being judged by a group of people who everybody was afraid of. They were thugs, criminals, fighters – but they were all Croatians.

I went back into the coffee shop to have another coffee. Mato, a big very tough criminal, was there. Everyone was afraid of him, but I was lucky to be in his good books.

He put a hand on my shoulder and told me, "Mario, your grandfather needs you. Your country needs you. Choose carefully what you are going to do next."

I got my coffee, and I went to the army barracks.

Boy to Adult, Dreamer to Soldier

"I saw a million lights on the horizon flashing, like a thousand lighthouses."

Why did I decide to go to the army barracks? Over the past few months, I'd seen the military barracks emptied of recruits and replaced with more and more reserves. This was replicated across Croatia.

Until the day he kicked me out of the house, my father had always tried to instil more responsibility in me. For example, he'd tell me, "You need to come to work earlier", "You need to listen to your superiors." You need to do this, you need to do that.

There was a lot of fear in me about what would happen if I didn't go to the barracks. I knew the federal state of Yugoslavia still existed and the police were still around. I didn't know what to expect, but I did know there were blockades manned by Croatian Police all across the city. There was a small nucleus of a Croatian

Army – just the beginning, just a few people with Kalashnikov AK-47s.

I knew I needed to go, even though I wasn't happy about it. Firstly, my heart was breaking into pieces and it felt like the feeling would last forever. The girl I loved had gone into the unknown and I was realising now I would probably never see her again.

As I was sitting on a bus driving to the army barracks, I saw the exodus – shops being emptied and people leaving in cars full of suitcases. You could cut the tension in the air with a knife. A storm was coming, but you didn't know when or how. It was all unknown.

We arrived at the barracks. There were a lot of reserve army guys about, guys in uniforms, unshaven with long beards, and a murky, angry look in their eyes, semi-drunk.

I thought to myself, "This is not Federal Army. Something terrible is happening. And there are a lot of us who've been picked up in a city to report to duty."

One very brief moment, a colonel came up to me and says, "Comrade Bekes, please come forward." I was in civilian clothes. He said to me, "I want you to go into the city and buy me some smokes." He then whispered, "Go slowly and gently, and do not rush back."

I replied, "But I need to stay in the army barracks."

He said to me, "Just go and buy me smokes."

I said, "That's going take at least hour to come back, you know what I mean? I don't know if this is a trick. Is this a joke?"

I was let out of the barracks as they went on high alert. The T55, T84, and T72 tanks had been positioned at every gate. Heavy machine guns and ammunition were being carried. Trucks were leaving loaded with equipment, bags and uniforms, and logistics were been taken out.

The barracks had been stripped of the main recruits and replaced with more motivated army reservists with heavy weapons from Serbia, happy to do damage to places that weren't their home. My city had several army barracks close to the hospitals and public market. There were also a couple of army training grounds outside the city. Again, the army reserves were there – with tanks, heavy artillery and multiple rocket launchers pointing towards the city.

As I was heading away from the barracks, a train with empty carriages stopped in the middle of the road, blocking my path. As I walked past the train, a Croatian police officer stopped me and asked me where I was going. I told him I was going to buy smokes and told him who I was in response to his questions.

Another gentleman came up to me near the train barricades – I recognised him as being a policeman from my city, who everyone knew. He said to me, "Your grandfather is a good man," and I said, "Yes, he is."

He told me, "Don't go back to the barracks. Go home. I want to see you tomorrow morning at the police station. Ask for me."

I was in shock. Yet again, I didn't know what to do. I was surprised, I was afraid.

It took me hour and a half to walk home. I was hungry and opened the fridge, which was empty except for jam and old bread.

I walked downstairs to the coffee shop, ordered an espresso and just sat there. Imagine yourself in my shoes. Imagine being eighteen and in just 24 hours the world you knew stopped existing. I was enjoying the coffee in that coffee shop, but I felt like my life had no purpose anymore. I didn't know where my parents were. I had no clue – they didn't even call me, they just left a message.

My grandfather was walking down the street. He was retired and very well-respected, despite the fact he worked for the communist Secret Police. He came up to me in the café and said, "Come on, let's go for walk."

I said, "Grandfather, I just can't. You know what I mean. I don't know what's happening."

He just said, "You're going to be okay."

He was a man of few words. He knew a number of my family

had forbidden love. They had married Serbians, and society has started rejecting these 'mixed marriages', as they were called then.

We just walked down the street, me and him. On a corner, opposite my building, I noticed a large group of women. They started praying loudly.

I remember it had been a beautiful, bright day until suddenly the sunset became dark. It was like the sky was becoming red, with dark, black clouds and stripes going through the red sky. I said goodbye to my grandfather, bought some food and went upstairs.

I was eating on the balcony and watched how the ladies were praying. It was very late, with a little bit of light on the horizon slowly disappearing into the night.

In the direction my balcony faced, there was a small village that was divided by Serbs and Croats. They had barricades between themselves. I knew the Federal Army had tanks and equipment positioned between the Croatian Police and the Serbs.

Everything was escalating so quickly. I can't even explain how quickly this happened. In just a few months, neighbours, families and friends started turning against each other. The drums of war were beating every single day on the TV, on the radio and in the newspapers.

As I was eating my sandwich on my balcony, the city was falling into dark night. The red sky was just dispersing. I saw a million lights on the horizon flashing, like a thousand lighthouses. I was just thinking that light appearing and disappearing was not normal. It reminded me of something else. I tried not to think about it anymore.

Then I heard a sound, and a second. It was like thunder from the lights on the horizon. Hundreds of the heavy artillery pieces, multiple rocket launchers, mortars – who knows what – started shelling the city. As the first shell hit a building, the screams started. People were screaming and crying everywhere.

It was a total bombardment. It only lasted two or three minutes but it was so intense. I sat there on the balcony in shock. I looked down to see people on the street bleeding and covered with cuts. Cars were on fire, roofs of buildings had exploded, and balconies were falling apart. Ladies were holding their heads, screaming and cursing at the same time. There were no men on the streets, just the women praying. There wasn't even one bullet you could see that someone was carrying that could have provoked this.

I ran downstairs to treat people and see if I could help. As soon as the fire brigades and ambulance appeared, I spotted the lights flashing again. The bombardment started once more. In military terms, this is called terrorism – when an ambulance comes to assist the wounded, and the bombardment continues. They knew what they were doing, as they had little helpers in the buildings communicating with them. They were using flashlights, phones and who knows what.

That night, the war had started – and from this very moment, life would be full of horror, suffering, sadness, tears, pain and nothing else.

Blood-Soaked Soil

"Nobody can prepare you for this, even if you are a trained soldier."

That night, blood was all over the ground, smeared on the concrete, splattered on the roads, leaving its mark on everybody forever.

After the shelling stopped, I went into the coffee shop because I knew there was something going on there as I could smell cooking. These boys knew what they were doing, so I looked for Mato.

He told me, "You. Tomorrow morning. You're gonna report to the police station."

I said, "Yes, I will."

While I was talking to him, I saw some older guys out in the street. Some big dicks, party members like my dad, had secretly got their weapons from the government over the past few months. These weapons that had cost the government so much were now being returned. I saw all sorts of different versions of AK-47's from Bulgaria and Romania, and Russian Spagin or 'Papasha' (PK machine pistols) from the Second World War. Imagine how ridiculous it was to believe that we were going to fight the third most powerful army in Europe at that time with light infantry weapons. Somehow we did.

These people were supposed to keep the weapons to help them instigate things for democracy, including rallies and barricades. I wondered how it was possible that these people had got their weapons secretly, after spending their entire lives talking of independence and how we needed to go to war. After the shelling, they were the first ones to go into the coffee shop and give their weapons back. To whom, you may ask? To us, a band of brothers? Just kids from the suburb? Ask yourself why. It was for the simple reason that they were afraid of the shelling and destruction. When they saw blood and dead bodies, they were the first ones to hide under their wives' skirts.

As if I was not afraid? Like I didn't realise the Yugoslav People's Army were shelling from the army barracks, and had surrounded villages using all types of artillery? In particular, they used multiple rocket launchers that could fire thirty-two rockets per salvo from one truck. Of course I was afraid – not that I had anyone to tell. I was naïve, young, filled with anger and rage at seeing the destruction caused, knowing that they (the Serbian rebels and Yugoslav Federal Army) were celebrating while we were breathing fear.

All I saw was the blood flowing on the street, while the fire brigades tried to clean up and ambulance crews picked up the body parts lying around.

The night was filled with fear. I didn't know what to do, so I spent the night in the coffee shop with these boys. I didn't know these guys were soon going to start defending my country.

All I knew was that it was the beginning of the end of the life I'd dreamt of. There was a new life ahead of me – a very different life. I only knew I needed to survive because I had nowhere to go. I didn't know where my parents were. The girl I loved had gone. I was now on my own, with a very ill grandfather and his wife to take care of. So I found a purpose.

I knew deep inside me that the dark blood flowing on the concrete and soil was just the start of more suffering. Nobody can prepare you for this, even if you are a trained soldier. There's no book, no video. There's no manual that can prepare you for such atrocities against your own kind. Military manuals are all well and good until the first bullet is fired. Everybody has a plan before they get punched in the face.

You suddenly needed to accept that everything you were seeing had become 'normal'. But it was *not* normal. I saw men crying, women weeping and children running in a circle as they'd been deafened by the shelling.

I knew that the only thing I had was myself. I knew I needed to adapt, and it was down to me to do it. Whatever was coming, it was coming. I didn't know how it was going to come, but I knew that it would only take one shell landing in my vicinity. Regardless of where I was, that would mean my life was over. Dozens of people suffered the ultimate fate that night, even the old lady praying with her rosaries. You can't adjust yourself overnight to these events. You just can't.

Evolution gives us key survival instincts we need to follow. We have five senses to see, feel, smell, touch and hear. War is all about this – you need all five to keep yourself alive. You are constantly asking, *Can you see it? Can you smell it? Can you hear it? Can you feel it? Can you touch it? Can you taste it?*

I know – you may think tasting isn't that important, but it is when there's the potential for gas poisoning or chemical and biological warfare. You need all five senses working on full power.

I started listening to my intuition, not just the training I'd had. Many people had been in the Army during peaceful times and they forgot their skills, they relaxed. In the Army, you repeat the same action over and over again – not to become perfect, but for the skill to become habitual. Perhaps that is a key element of surviving – making sure it isn't my blood flowing down to the street or soaking the soil beneath me.

It's great to talk about positive thinking at a time when everything is okay – not perfect, but okay – when there's some hope. But suddenly, you are being confined to your city, divided by the blockades with curfews, and there is constant fear and uncertainty amongst the people, day and night. What was strange was that during this time, in the other part of my city, people went out like normal.

Initially, the shelling was very selective. In other parts of the city, people really were carrying on as if nothing was happening. But that soon came to an end. War was spreading like cancer, with death, destruction and craziness amongst the people.

The Ten Commandments

"Thou shalt not kill."

Church was not very glamorous and did not play a role in Croatian society in the '70s and '80s. However, in 1990, when the Croatian uprising was gathering pace and the first democratic elections took place, there were priests everywhere, in every corner of society. They gave blessings, preached and also made a call to arms.

This didn't make sense to me. A few years earlier, I'd been watching the *Ten Commandments* movie, which told us that 'Thou shalt not kill'. Now, a priest was coming over to people with tender rosaries and gently calling people to arms.

So yes, they had become tainted. The Roman Catholic Church in Croatia wanted their properties back that had been nationalised after the Second World War. Many priests had been executed by communists, the Secret Police and the Army. The Croatian Roman Catholic Church was always on side of the Croatian government, the Axis forces of Italy and Germany, and the monarchy. I understood all of this, but couldn't understand why the priests were publicly glorifying war after teaching us not to kill.

Every protest had a priest involved as part of the call to arms. I felt nationalism waking inside me. Maybe I was just being young and naive, with no understanding of events from twenty or fifty years ago. I just wanted to be loved, have a family, to grow up and do my bit for society.

Priests were involved from the first days of the war and were later attached to all army units. They used to give rosaries to the soldiers. They were blessing us before we went into combat. I was just anxious. *"If we don't do this, they will do that to us? We need to fight for freedom."*

How do I relate to the church today? Many years afterwards, my beautiful son was born. Unfortunately, due to war injuries and various circumstances I can't have children, so he was conceived through IVF.

My wife and I decided to baptise him. We came back to the Croatian Roman Catholic Church, where they told me my son was not good enough as he was conceived 'against the God's will'. Everything in my life just fell apart. I felt completely betrayed by the same people who used to send me into combat with rosaries around my neck. How could my son not be good enough?

The moral I draw from this is regardless how big or small you are or your belief in God, you need to find your own faith. It is dangerous for someone else to introduce you to a faith because you can become a puppet.

Does God exist? He does, but you need to find out on your own how God exists for you. Through the destructions and miseries of war, I learnt for myself that God exists. This was proved time and time again to me.

I was not always brave. At first, I felt very afraid. Then the madness of war gave me some kind of injection and I became reckless. I didn't care whether I lived or died.

When I was on my own and in dangerous situations, I used to pray to God. I remember saying to him, "God, just let me live through this hell today. I promise you, just look after me. I'll do some good things in my life."

Training

*"You don't know what dying is 'til you die.
And when you die, you don't even know you've died."*

The day after the first shelling, I woke up alone. Evidence of the night before was on the concrete, asphalt, grass and bricks falling from the buildings. It made a powerful statement and sent a message of the misery coming.

It was terrifying to see all the blood stains on the asphalt. People were walking slowly. They would stop for a second or two to take it all in, then chat to each other. It was like everybody wanted life to go back to normal, like it had been the day before. That last night was just an episode, a misunderstanding. I knew it was no misunderstanding.

I knew what the Yugoslav People's Army were capable of doing. I knew that the Serbs in the occupied villages were supported by the Army. I knew that war was just waiting to happen. Still there were people, particularly the older generations, who somehow believed that everything was going to be okay. After all, for years everybody had been taught that the Army was there to make everybody feel safe, secure and to protect our way of life.

I went into the coffee shop, where all the older tough boys hung out with their murky, adventurous pasts. I had my coffee sitting with my boys. I had a deep respect for many of them, as they weren't A-grade students or those with successful parents. All these kids who I went to primary school with had decided that it was time to do something, to defend and protect innocent people and our lifestyle.

Eventually, I sat on a bus and travelled fourteen stops to report to the general who had sent me out for smokes.

"Mario, you've arrived at the perfect time," he said. I just looked at him – I didn't understand. "The bus for the Ministry of the Interior Special Forces Training Centre is about to leave and you are going to be on it." I wasn't sure about it, but he said, "Well, you have a choice. Stay here or you join up. Aren't you Croatian?"

I said, "Yes, of course I am."

The Ministry of the Interior was Croatia's government agency for security and defence, and their training camp was at a place called Kumrovec. Waiting for the bus, I was chatting to the other boys, who were all around my age and quite similar to me. I noticed that nobody was married or had kids. Most had fallen foul of the police at some stage and had been arrested or put in prison. I couldn't care less.

I saw people rushing to catch trains out of the city. People were fleeing, and this was just the beginning. The true exodus would happen in November.

I noticed that the police uniforms were changing. New camouflage uniforms with Croatian insignia were slowly replacing the Yugoslav uniforms.

Suddenly my name was being called. "Mario, it is time."

I was so afraid of what was coming. I drank coffee all day and took some whiskey to have with me on the bus. I didn't really understand why they chose us, but I knew it was because we were enthusiastic, adventurous and patriotic. They also knew we were afraid.

Training

The bus drove for six hours into the Croatian countryside, where a training centre had been established for the Special Forces. We started drinking the moment we got off the bus. Instructors were everywhere – calling our names, giving out uniforms and weapons.

My drill instructor looked at me and said, "How old are you?" I told him I was almost nineteen (well, I would be in three months). He then said, "What's your weight?" I said, "Around 89 kilos." He replied, "Son, we're going to give you something beautiful."

In Chuck Norris movies and *Rambo*, everyone has a heavy machine gun they hold in one hand with the bullets in the other. I thought I'd get something like that. I was wrong. I got a German MG42, which was a very heavy machine gun. It shot 7.9-millimetre bullets and fired 1,500 rounds per minute. That's a level of destruction that is hard to describe. Then there's the deafening sound it makes.

I got the machine gun and my uniform, and we started training the following day. We were more of a rag tag outfit with different colour uniforms. We had bullet-proof vests, but I have no idea where they came from – possibly the Vietnam War. Croatians who were living overseas had been flooding Croatia with military equipment.

During the seven days at the training centre, we learnt a lot. One thing nobody could teach us was how to control the fear. Nobody can tell you what to do when it comes to the worst moment in your life and you are staring death in the face. Nobody can tell you how much you can endure as a human.

There was only one reason for all this training – and that was to put us into action, as Croatia didn't have an army yet. On one side there were the rebels and the Yugoslav People's Army. On the other side there was us, the newly-formed Police Force. Some military units were beginning to be formed, and then there were the Special Forces. We were to counter-attack as the first and last line of defence.

I wasn't afraid of dying because I didn't know what dying was. You don't know what dying is until you die. And when you die, you don't even know you've died. Imagine how hypocritical this is. Every society that drafts soldiers puts them through a medical, looking for healthy human beings – and you are proud that you are healthy and can serve the Army. What you cannot avoid is the fact that, in war, people will die. All that health, all those years of mothers and fathers looking after you as a child means nothing. The moment you step onto the battlefield or into the trenches, it's likely you will die.

In seven days, we learnt how to destroy a tank, how to make a Molotov cocktail, how to use knives, how to act at night and how to create an ambush. It was a quick crash course.

On the seventh day, we were told we were going back to our home city to pass the knowledge onto newly formed units. I didn't know I was going to be posted into units of people I knew from my suburb. Those people were heroes for me as they had stayed at home. They didn't want to go. They wanted to defend and protect their country, just like I did.

During my time at the Special Forces centre, the news was becoming darker and darker. The Yugoslav People's Army Air Force was bombing left, right and centre across Croatia.

The barracks were shooting everybody who went past. As they were mainly positioned opposite hospitals and schools, it made it difficult for many cities to function. There were so many atrocities being carried out. I don't want to talk about them, there were so many.

The anger and rage inside of me kept growing. I couldn't understand why civilians should be targeted in every possible way. They were being overwhelmed by the Yugoslav People's Army. The names of dead people, aged from 0 to 100, were everywhere.

On my eighth day, I returned to Osijek and reported for duty.

The Summer of 1991

*"Despite all the beautiful colours of summer,
everything around us had become grey and dark."*

It was July, summer 1991. Summer usually represents the time of freedom, short sleeves, sun, fun, barbecues, going to the beach, holidays and falling in love. It's a happy time of year, especially in comparison to the cold Croatian winters full of frost and snow.

The summer of 1991 was much like that for most people on our planet. However, for me, it couldn't be more different. I'd just come back from my training to a city that was being shelled every day and night. More people had fled. Most people I knew from school had left, their parents trying to protect them in other parts of the country and beyond.

Despite this, the city kept some spirit. It was amazing to see how people kept functioning day by day with the constant shelling. People would gather to clean the smashed windows and burning cars. The emergency services kept operating, as did public transport. Coffee shops were still open, people still went for drinks and saw friends. Everyone also understood while we were under siege, there was only one road out.

That summer, I saw how one country was born from the ashes, literally from nothing. When we were part of Yugoslavia, Croatia hadn't had an army. Now, we did. Every city and village started creating units. I don't know how they were formed or who was giving the orders – I suspect the President from the capital city. Others were closer to the decision-making process than me. I was just a boy who had stopped dreaming. That part of me had been taken away, along with my first love. Suddenly, I'd become a very serious young man who understood that this summer would always stay the summer I'd want to forget.

No matter how much warmth the sun provided, I saw that part of my life was being erased. Everything I'd learnt at school, every belief that had been drilled into me and every other child in Croatia and the wider Yugoslavia was disappearing. There was no carefree summer on the river, in the pool, chasing the girls. I knew things were very serious now.

As I have mentioned, until now Croatia did not have an army – it had the police: the regular police and the Special Forces. They were armed, mainly with Kalashnikovs, some heavy infantry weapons and rocket launchers. The rest of our equipment was home-made. Trucks had been converted and painted in camouflage colours. On top they would place a Flak 20mm single, double or even triple barrelled gun. It was a very popular weapon.

Our strongest weapon was our courage, eagerness and desire to fight for independence. With the shock we witnessed every day, we were becoming a band of brothers, united by a common goal. We were fighting for freedom, democracy and peace. We also knew that many of our friends were on the other side and in the enemy ranks.

Despite all the beautiful colours of summer, everything around us had become grey and dark. I can't explain that feeling, but it must be something that happens when war starts. Even the weather you see is changing. Your eyes start seeing something different. Is it a chemical reaction in the brain? I don't know, I can't explain it. It felt like a mystery.

You could feel the atmosphere full of fear, anxiety, adrenaline, anger and sadness. It is bleak when people are separated by religion. Those of us who wanted to fight for the independence of Croatia also fought for revenge, for having our freedom taken away.

Kill the Fear or Die

*"Being the youngest one doesn't mean that
you are the bravest."*

It was my first official day in the war. I was slowly walking around the apartment in the early morning. The phone rang – one of those big plastic old phones that was considered sophisticated back then. A female voice told me, "Mario, pick up your equipment. Pick up your weapon. The truck is coming to pick you up."

I had my uniform on and thought I looked really smart. It was a camouflage uniform with military boots and a shiny belt. I caught my reflection in the mirror and, for a brief moment, I truly believed the Army was going to be like a *Rambo* movie. I had my MG42 machine gun and I was going to win freedom for my country in one day. How mistaken I was.

I picked up my equipment and prepared to walk out the door of my home. I wished I could see my parents one more time, but there was nobody else there. The apartment was silent. I locked the windows, checked that the oven wasn't leaking gas and that the electricity was off.

Then I stepped outside. I saw my neighbour preparing to leave the city with his family. Instead of respect or fear, he looked at me as if to say, *"Is this guy going to draft me to the Army?"* I saw in his eyes he didn't want a part of it. He was older than me, in his mid-thirties. I was eighteen.

He shook my hand in an 'I'll see you when I see you' kind of way, and said, "Mario, I don't know what to say."

"Be safe with your family," I said.

The big, low truck with grey markings appeared in front of my building. I recognised it and the driver from a local moving and furniture company. My unit didn't even have a military truck.

The unit contained people I knew, which was great until they stepped into uniform. I knew I'd had more training than anybody else, but they were the tough guys I used to admire. They would walk the streets and everyone would run away from them. People respected them, but hated them, too.

I saw how few cars were in the parking lot. Normally the place would be full of cars in front of every block. It was designed this way so people could easily see into all the apartments and report back to authorities.

The streets were quiet, except for a few people in the coffee shop. It was quieter than it used to be. Windows were covered with sticky tape to prevent shattering from mortars, artillery and rockets. Sandbags protected the basements, which had quickly been converted into makeshift refuges when the shelling started.

Everyone in the truck greeted me. I was the youngest one there. I looked at everyone's faces. Some were happy, some looked afraid and most seemed to have had a few drinks already. I was anxious. I couldn't wait to get into combat, but I didn't know what to expect. I smelt the summer and the sun getting brighter, but those dark feelings inside me were still very dark indeed.

Trucks were slowly departing to the suburbs. We drove to the city centre, where we were due to report at the police station. We saw few people or cars. It was all very unusual.

The police station was opposite the main train station. I saw buses full of women, children and some men fleeing the city, a scene that was to be repeated until November. On that day I saw the first armoured train had been converted. Volunteer soldiers of the Croatian Army were arriving by the handful.

We all went into the police station to find the backyard covered and lights turned off. It was daytime but the corridors were still kept dark. The lack of lights made the building less visible from the air. Lights gave the enemy the opportunity to see and orientate themselves. My city was very flat, so you were able to see lights from kilometres away.

People were wearing a lot of different uniforms. Some were camouflage like mine, and others a blue-ish grey – the first uniforms of the newly formed Croatian Police.

We were directed into a big room where officers used to play exercise and basketball or soccer. We were told we could go out to buy smokes and coffee, but we had to be back in half an hour. Of course, I went with the crowd, my band of brothers. I wanted to parade around. I wanted people to notice me in uniform, looking tough and ready for the action. How naive and stupid I was.

Once we returned from the coffee shop opposite the police station, we noticed there was some unclaimed equipment on the floor that didn't seem to belong to anyone. Roll call came. It consisted more of battle groups rather than a single unit. During the roll call, it was confirmed that the unclaimed equipment on the floor belonged people who were missing.

The full reality of everything hit me in that moment. This was not a *Rambo* movie, not a Chuck Norris one-man army. I was afraid, and felt the fear coursing through my bones. A top-ranking officer told me, "Mario, kill the fear or die." But how do you know how to kill the fear? I didn't know much about fear. A few weeks ago, my biggest fear had been getting poor grades at school, or how I was going to kiss the girl. Now, I had the fear of combat, dying in combat, the horror of war and the destruction it causes. How do you know how to get rid of that fear?

We were told we were going to drive in trucks, a couple of four-wheel drive vehicles, filled with different battle groups. We were to report to the village of Ernestinovo – which had a command post for that region, similar to reporting to the police station in my city. I couldn't understand why we were going to drive through villages that were likely to have people who were definitely not loyal to the Croatian Government. They were not supportive of Croatian Independence and democracy, and they were likely to call some of the villages with Yugoslav People's Army units, stationed together with Serbian rebels. It seemed illogical. We didn't have military trucks or armoured vehicles. All we had was hearts and souls.

While I was away for coffee and smoke, I didn't hear what the commanding officers had been talking about. I was not a commanding officer, just a police officer of the Special Forces. I had heard the night before that there was a huge fight in Ernestinovo, and that whoever was defending that village for us had sustained heavy casualties. The attack had stopped, but the casualties were there. Our job was to replace them for four days until another group was going to replace us. These people needed to have a break and recuperate.

We went to pick up more equipment, hand grenades and anti-tank grenades. I was picking up all the belts I could, with the same 7.9mm ammunition as my MG42 machine gun. I had no way of counting the 500 bullets on each belt. I just knew I needed to replace the belt frequently due to the ferocity and speed of how many bullets the gun could spit out. It was unbelievable.

I did have a colleague or 'aide' to help me hold the ammunition belt during fighting, replenish my ammunition and support me with other duties. He was a man in his forties who had recently lost members of his family through the aggression of the Serbian forces. He was vindictive and a very sour, angry man. He always told me, "You just shoot. I'll make a sure that you have all bullets possible."

It was pointless to say, 'I do not want to go on the mission', regardless of how afraid I was. I just kept being told, "Kill the fear or die." I was the youngest one, and everybody looked at me with a smile in their eyes. I think most of them were proud of me for joining up. Being the youngest one didn't mean I was the bravest, though.

We walked back towards the truck and joined four other vehicles, with sixty or seventy of us together. We travelled for around two and a half hours to the village of Ernestinovo with its command post. I had heard about the village, but had never explored it. Not having a car meant that I hadn't explored the surrounding countryside outside my city. I didn't know where any of the villages actually were.

The Village

"I caught a glimpse of the tank's commanding officer. He was eating an apple, sitting on the top of the tank as it charged down the concrete road towards us."

Ernestinovo is a very small village, beautifully designed with a major intersection and the main road going through the middle. It was a quiet, artistic village, famous for its annual wood sculpture exhibition. People had been happy living here – however, they felt the brunt of the war much more than my city, as they were surrounded by villages occupied by rebels and the People's Army.

We parked in front of the command post. There was a school nearby. We all went inside to relax. I was conscious of so many different types of uniforms, units and weapons. Many of the weapons were not made in the in eighties or nineties, but relics of the Second World War.

The Croatian Army and Ministry of the Interior Special Forces had a liking for armoured vehicles, tanks, infantry, transport and aircraft vehicles. In fact, they liked all forms of vehicle that could offer some protection from bullets and shrapnel.

Then I saw how ingenious people were. There were no tanks made in the backyards and garages, but armoured vehicles, yes, absolutely. They would take the chassis of a five-ton truck and add 2cm thick steel plated armour with openings to poke weapons through. They looked pretty good painted in camouflage, and were actually quite powerful, although nothing compared to the People's Army weapon systems and properly armoured vehicles. However, we believed in what had been made and that it would provide some type of protection. We could imagine all the rebels and Yugoslav Army laughing when they saw these through their binoculars. What they couldn't see was that every vehicle was made with pride and dignity. Personally, I couldn't believe we were going to war in these trucks.

We went into a classroom, thinking about what was going to happen, what was going to be done and how. Then I heard a new sound, a different type of shelling. This was mortar fire, falling sporadically around the village. From my knowledge, the enemy was measuring distance and marking homes or objects. They didn't know exactly where we were, so they tried to cover the entire length of the road. They knew we were going to start moving to the neighbouring village of Laslovo. It was only a few kilometres from Ernestinovo, but it was through an open field. In war conditions, you were like a sitting duck if you were on the road. We knew that when we needed get to Laslovo later that day.

For a few hours while it was quiet we relaxed in the classroom and I fell asleep for just a brief moment. It felt like any other day, with the smell of the flowers, green trees and lush vegetation around the school.

While we were relaxing, some units who had prepared armoured vehicles in front of the school were bringing in their ammunition and necessities. Suddenly out of the blue, an alarm was raised and we rushed outside to where the handmade armoured truck was.

We climbed inside. It was very dark and cold in the truck. This was it.

We started traveling. As soon as we came out of the village and into the open, all I felt was the *tick, tick, tack* of bullets hitting the handmade armour. Some of the guys pulled out smokes. As well as the sporadic ricocheting of bullets, you could hear mortars falling. They fell with a deep sound that was an almost operatic *boom, boom, boom*.

The drive was quick and suddenly we'd stopped in Laslovo. People came to speak to the driver, recognising him and the vehicle. I was completely unaware anything was happening. As soon as we came out, the shooting started from every possible side. I couldn't see anybody. It's not like in the movies where you can easily see the enemy. I didn't know what was going on.

Everybody was looking for cover. Some went into ditches in front of houses, some stayed in the truck and others ran into nearby homes. Interestingly, we all knew where each other went. A few minutes later, we organised ourselves on one side of the street, the side that had not been shelled or shot up.

It was a terrifying experience to see homes with no roofs. Wires had been cut, and blood, bandages and bullet cases were strewn everywhere. As we walked about 1.5km down the street, there were three mortars being operated by women who were selflessly trying to stop the attack from the next village, where the rebels were. Bullets were raining down on us and I couldn't believe the courage of these young women, or the fact they were still smiling when they saw us.

We progressed to the command post, where their commanding officer spoke to our commanding officer. They divided us into groups. My group was to take position in the centre of the village on the road. They said that there was an impending attack from one side. There was one concrete road and a small bridge that hadn't been hit, so it was thought that was where the attack would come from.

As I was rushing into position, I saw everybody's fear for the first time. Bullets were flying, I didn't know what was going on. I tried to keep as low as possible. I tried to stay undercover, crawling with all that ammunition and the heavy machine gun. Behind me, my aide was crawling so slowly. I saw that his eyes were full of tears.

Eventually we reached our position. It was our only possible position as we couldn't retreat into the village. We had to cut off the village on the main road that we had come through. Were we going to be stuck forever? I knew that the Croatian Army didn't have much manpower or equipment to help.

For a moment, it felt like I was in a mini-Stalingrad. I'd learnt about Stalingrad at school – this huge battle where Germany lay siege to the city of Stalingrad in southern Russia. The Germans were fierce and relentless – taking two million casualties. No mercy was shown to anyone.

A few times in this war, I felt that same horrific feeling, with goosebumps covering every centimetre of my skin. Were we going to end like Stalingrad? Is that what falling would look like? Of course, you can't compare the scale and size of the village to the city of Stalingrad.

I remember that we lay low, and waited and waited. It was 4pm. The sun was slowly going down. You could feel the sweat was drying up on your skin, and there was the dirty smell of the uniform. The other clear smell was the cleaning oil on your weapon.

I prepared my position and studied everything about it. There were big gaps between me and the other soldiers to my left and right. Of course, my 13 kilo machine gun and its 5,000 bullet machine gun could be in the first position to attack. It was just me and my aide. A few metres from me, the other boys were digging deep and hiding themselves so they could have a smoke. Some were lying on their backs and looking up at the sky.

Looking around me, everybody was from the same neighbourhood or high school. Nobody's parents were politicians or company directors, from positions of privilege. I wondered, how come there wasn't anyone well educated amongst us? Of course, well educated people don't fight on a front line. Their parents hide their children and take advantage of their good positions in government and companies. They would not send their children into a war. It was just us, ordinary Mr Nobodies.

We waited. Who knows what was going through everybody's heads? Even I can't remember, but I do know I was afraid. I needed to kill that fear as the bullets were flying over our heads.

Then I heard the boisterous sound of a tank. I heard the T-55, charging at full speed towards us from 700 metres away. I could smell the diesel from its exhaust pipes.

When the tank was around 300 metres away, I caught a glimpse of the tank's commanding officer. He was eating an apple, sitting on the top of the tank as it charged down the concrete road towards us.

'Mum' – The Last Word Every Man Says

"I will not lie, I was not afraid – I was petrified."

I never properly saw the tank charging towards us. I never saw infantry behind the tank running and rushing into combat. I just knew one thing, and only one thing – that this could be the very last day of my life.

As everybody was trying to see what was happening in front of us, the shooting began and continued to intensify. We waited. We knew we need to wait.

I was wondering, "Okay, we can deal with the infantry, but what about the tank?"

Then behind the tank, we saw the two-armed personnel vehicles. They must be full of soldiers. I heard my radio (or was it someone else's?) – somehow somebody arrived with an RPG (rocket-propelled grenade).

The tank was only 100 metres away. I saw the flame from the RPG flying out of the tube, and then I saw the tank had been stopped. The track had been broken. We only had one rocket and the man who shot it said, "Guys, now everything's on you. See you later."

All hell broke loose. All I saw in front of me were enemy soldiers running, screaming. I will not lie: I was not afraid – I was petrified. I was praying to God simultaneously – "God, I just want to survive this day. Please let me survive this day. Be beside me." I had the feeling I was not going to see daylight after this.

Somebody flipped me onto my back. He said, "Mario, what are you waiting for? Do it!"

I just got behind my machine gun and looked at my aide. His eyes were bloody. I couldn't tell whether he was crying or angry. I started spraying bullets the entire length of the front line. That terrible sound of the MG42 echoed and I could feel the heat from the barrel as hundreds of bullets screamed into the infinity of the space ahead of me. I saw dust lifting in front of me and all I felt was rage and the desire to survive. Kill or to be killed was never a question – it was an automatic response.

After maybe twenty or thirty seconds, the bullets jammed. I opened the gun quickly and cleaned it. I started to fire again and again. Everybody was screaming at me, "Stop it! Stop it!" I couldn't hear because the sound of the machine gun was deafening. It was like a chainsaw on steroids.

The attack started and stopped in maybe three minutes. I saw a few of my soldiers were wounded – one in the shoulder, another in the leg and one in the arse. Nobody knows how he was hit there!

We had some hand grenades to throw lying in front of us, so we threw them. There were a few screams from all sides.

I heard somebody calling for his mother – "Mum, Mum, hold me."

I know that my stomach was shaking. I can't really explain the feeling, but it was genuinely shaking.

My colleagues were looking at me saying, "You've done so well. You've done so well." We were congratulating and complimenting each other.

Village of the Damned

"This boy was becoming a man...
I was holding my finger on the trigger of a piece of
machinery invented to take a life."

I was looking around me the moment the fight stopped, which did not last for long. I could smell the grass, the leaves and the soil. My hand was burnt because I did not have any protective gloves to change the machine gun barrel. I could not feel anything.

I could not believe it was over – but most importantly, I could not understand how easy it was for life to end. That day, life ended for quite a few. Militaries around the world have created all this weaponry, equipment and everything else just to destroy life and property.

I was thinking to myself, *"I wonder what my enemy was thinking before he was charging toward us? Did they say goodbye to their families? What did they eat? What were they thinking? How did they feel? Did they have hatred inside? Anger?"* I'm not sure, but I'd guess they knew this was all very real.

From the moment the combat and battle started, the only thing in your head was to survive, to inflict damage on the enemy. I know I was thinking this. I'm sure my enemies were thinking exactly the same thing. I know that I survived. I know people died. I saw them – I heard their screams, on the ground, in the bushes and behind the trees. I don't know what happened to them. I realised that after this battle, maybe in the next moment, I was going to be the one who was going to scream. I was going to feel numb, maybe open my eyes and perhaps see clouds one last time.

I knew that, despite my best efforts, I wanted to see my parents. I wanted to see them, regardless of how upset I was that they'd dumped me like a dog, how abandoned I felt. There were so many emotions going around in my head.

Then I remembered, when I was very young, I'd been told that there is a moment when a boy becomes a man. Well, aged almost nineteen, this was my moment. It was due to one thing – I was holding my finger on the trigger of a piece of machinery invented to take life.

People had their heads buried in the ground due to the fear. Fear was real. Danger was imminent.

I realised that my survival depended on the basic skills and senses given to me from birth. They were given to me by evolution. You can hear and see if your enemy is walking towards you. It's the same in business. You can see somebody walking towards you and tell whether they want to shake your hand, hug you or punch you. You can also smell people – it's amazing how far away you can smell alcohol, at least fifteen metres away. You can see a cigarette in the pitch dark from a kilometre away. Senses were my guidance from that very moment.

Nobody can prepare you on the horrors of war. It is not like the movies or documentaries. I saw people who had lost limbs and I prayed. "God, I do not want to finish up in a wheelchair. God, just let me survive one more night, one more night."

I promised God so many things that I can't even remember anymore. I know deep inside of me, I was afraid. I was afraid that

I was going to die on the ground in some God-forsaken village. I was going to be dead and have my life extinguished.

We were told to march towards Laslovo, and another group of soldiers would replace us there. We were told to find a place to relax and recuperate.

As I walked towards the village, I saw the dead bodies of Federal Army soldiers. The armoured personnel carrier was burning silently, with the awful smell of charred bodies. Everybody was just walking past looking at those dead bodies, the bullet casings and the weapons all around. Nobody was in a rush.

No-one said anything until we reached the end of the street. Most of the homes had been abandoned, except for a few people who'd been defending the village with some of the local Croatian Army units.

We walked into a newly-built house with two levels. We decided to go into the attic to relax, and so we would be able to see everything from the roof. I was arguing that this wasn't a good idea, but was told it was fine and to relax for a bit. There were twenty of us in the attic, and our other colleagues were in the house next door. We just sat there laughing.

The occasional shelling of mortars continued. *Boom, boom, boom.* Then silence again.

I remember one guy lifted the roof tiles to look out. "Everything is so quiet," he said.

It is rare that you can hear nothing at all, not even the birds singing or dogs barking. Somehow animals seem to have some kind of sixth sense and know when things are awry. Complete silence is usually a signal that bad things are about to happen.

We were passing some water and smokes around – then, the next moment a violent bombardment began. There were shots landing 200 metres away, with mortars, artillery and tanks. Shells began hitting the homes we were in. They were shooting house by house.

Mortars hit the roof as we started running downstairs to take position in the field at the front of the house. Unfortunately for everybody else, I was running first with my machine gun strapped over my back and got stuck in a doorway. I couldn't unstrap the gun, so the guys behind me were yelling at me to move. Eventually, they pushed the machine gun vertically and we all started falling down the stairs. The incident would have belonged in a slapstick comedy, if it hadn't been such a dire situation.

We became the casualties of our own stupidity. We shouldn't have been in the attic. The mortars were firing intensely. We felt the bombardment from the anti-tank cannons and artillery being levelled up at the homes, causing more direct hits.

They were not far away from us, maybe 700 metres in the nearby occupied village. The bombardment lasted around twenty minutes. We stopped counting the shells.

We were still looking each other in the eyes, having a smoke and cracking some jokes. But we knew there was fear amongst us. We knew things were dangerous, but our overwhelming feeling was one of anger. There was rage inside us, making us want to fight because of the destruction happening in front of our very eyes.

It was real. We couldn't run away from this. Chances to make a break for it were being destroyed with every single mortar and bullet. We knew there were going to be casualties.

We didn't know that the enemy was going to be so slow coming. They were slowly approaching the village through the field with its long grass. We had scouts telling us this on the radio. I never understood why they wanted that village so badly, but it was war and we knew we had nowhere to hide. There were no backup armies or planes – nothing but us, our knives, infantry and anti-tank weapons.

Then the bombing stopped.

Interestingly enough, they didn't attack us. We took positions in the long grass of the field and waited. We waited for almost an hour and nobody appeared. There was just the deadly silence as the sun slipped slowly beyond the horizon.

My very first day in a war was coming to an end. I wasn't hungry, I wasn't tired. I didn't know what was happening to me. A random thought came into my head. What was happening in other countries? Did they know there is a war here in Croatia? Did they know what we were fighting for, that we were dying here with nobody to help? Nobody could care less.

I knew there was psychological warfare going on through the TV, radio and newspapers. We didn't have a TV that day but we did have radios. We found them in the homes, still working. Most of the homes still had their furniture, with the last meal on a stove or kitchen table. Only the clothes were missing.

We heard on the radio how we were bravely defending this village, and how we had caused so much damage for the rebels and the Yugoslav People's Army. It said they had suffered many casualties – which they had, but not that many.

Then I realised that nobody from the media was there with us in the village. How could they possibly know what was going on? Radio was the only thing connecting us with the civilised world. We were like kids, sitting inside these homes, while guards were patrolling the corn and wheat fields around the village, waiting for something to happen.

We improvised a lot. It is hard to know how people are going to behave when faced with certain situations. Everybody was new to this. None of us had ever been in a war. We didn't know anything about dying, about killing, about being awake all day and all night.

I saw people drinking. You could see people were not thinking about the situation they were in. They were thinking about their wives, girlfriends and children. Me? I didn't know what was going through my head. I knew that I didn't have parents anymore – they didn't even have a clue where I was. They had no idea what was happening to me.

I stopped worrying about my situation and started to think about my girl, who I loved very much. We had been separated for some time now. She couldn't even reach me. I was thinking it would be foolish if I told her how I was defending Croatia, while she had gone to the country who supported the rebels and Federal

Yugoslav People's Army. I didn't think she would understand this. She had gone to a peaceful, quiet place where life was carrying on as per normal, while in my country everything was burning. Everything was on fire and destroyed by shelling.

Of course people would start drinking. I saw the cracks in people on the very first day. Stress, hands shaking, being absent when they were asked something, their eyes just staring through you.

We shared some cans of food. Nobody cared. In that moment, we had nothing – just each other.

That day, I learnt to take apart my machine gun and put it back together in just fifteen seconds. That's how familiar I had become with my weapon. I saw other guys frantically cleaning their weapons. You need to clean your weapon.

I had also learnt how to use it. I'd never fired it previously, and now I was repeating and repeating the actions of cleaning my weapon.

Repetition doesn't make you perfect. It makes things permanent.

Soon I was able to take apart and rebuild my gun in the pitch black, difficult terrains and terrible weather conditions. I knew my weapon inside out. I was depending on that weapon to protect me, protect my peace and my band of brothers. I knew that this gun was going to be my best friend. I didn't know how long for.

I thought back to this time last year, when I'd been enjoying the summer, swimming, chasing girls and larking about with my friends. Now I was sitting in this abandoned house, with this band of brothers I was now sharing my destiny with.

With darkness approaching, we received our duties – who was going to go on guard duty, and who was going to sleep? Again, that deadly silence hung across the village. It was pitch black, there were no lights, electricity, gas or water. Everything had been cut off. Everything had suddenly become so primitive.

We didn't have a proper line to defend. It was a village created on a T-shape axis with two main streets. There were no front lines, no trenches – just houses.

We knew the enemy was in front of us. We had heard rumours the Yugoslav People's Army had sent Special Forces to that area. They were enemy units that everybody feared, but we didn't. We were different. We knew that we were going to stick together and die together if necessary. We believed in a cause and, more than that, we knew we had nowhere to go – just that we were depending on each other.

A sound broke the silence. It was the quiet noise of a little radio in the corner of the room. Some of the guys came to me and said, "Listen, Mario, if you hear the ducks or dogs barking, that means they're coming."

In less than twelve hours, I had learnt so much about survival. The only reason I learned about survival was the fact that the situation was life or death. It was not about beliefs, purpose, politics or democracy any more. It was up to you to survive, to protect yourself and your guys around you. Okay we were a unit, but really we were just a group of guys. That's how we worked.

I was told that my guard duty was going to be between one and three o'clock in the morning. That's the worst time. Your body is just exhausted, you want to sleep. I tried to fall asleep during the evening and till midnight. I didn't have a watch or a wallet – I had nothing except my photo ID card from the Ministry of the Interior. This added extra fear that, if you were captured, they would know all about you. My mind was racing. I just couldn't fall asleep.

I was in the kitchen and there was a big clock on the wall. Everywhere in the house you could hear it ticking. I was in uniform with all my equipment on me. There were no pillows or sleeping bags – just your uniform, equipment, weapon and ammunition. The only thing I could find was a shiny, beige teddy bear. I found myself holding it so close to my heart that I felt a pain inside my chest.

I was holding the teddy bear as other guys were passing by me. There were candles on a table and you could still smell the burning amour, vehicles and bodies in the village. I put the bear under my head and tried to sleep, but my entire life was spinning in front of my eyes – my childhood, my first love, my parents, everything I'd experienced up to that day. Then I replayed that day – the first battle, the combat, the baptism by fire. Next, I felt the fear and anxiety. It was like a cold bead of sweat moving across my body.

Then one of the guys come into the room and said, "Mario, it's your turn."

I said, "What?"

He said, "You're going to do your guard duty." He explained to me what to do, then gave me the radio and some hand grenades.

There I was standing in front of the house, just staring out into the night, watching. All I could see was another guy doing exactly the same thing in the house opposite. There was a deadly silence. You just want to see the first light on the horizon.

Then I heard the ducks. I ran inside the house, waking everybody up to tell them the enemy was coming. Everyone got their weapons. Nobody came. We learned not to trust the ducks anymore.

As the time passed, first light began to slowly appear on the horizon. "God, I only need one more day. Thank you, God, I'm alive."

That morning we were replaced with a different unit and headed back to the city. When I arrived back in my city, I was the biggest hero. I told everyone what had happened and they didn't think it was possible. The boys came across to the coffee shop where I was, saying it was true.

I'd had my first day at war and was apparently already a hero. Allegedly, the story of my first day encouraged many people to be braver than they would have been otherwise.

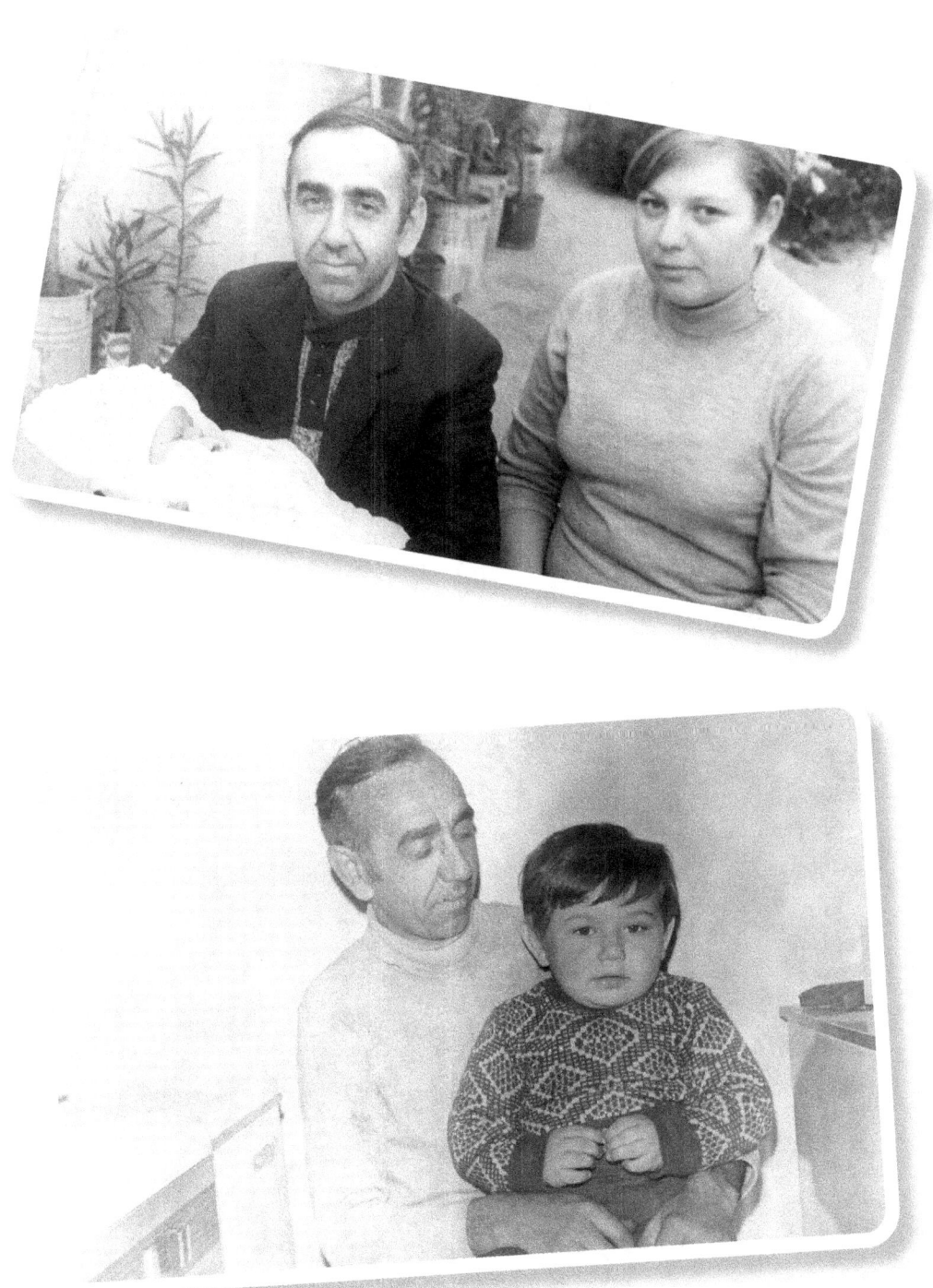

Grandparents and Insulin

"My adrenaline kicked in. I felt like I was flying and the fastest guy in the world."

I came back to my apartment and opened the door. The unit had an unusual smell that I couldn't explain. Perhaps it was because the unit had been shut up for thirty hours, and there had been no humans inside.

Then I realised that I didn't have any money, not one dollar in my pocket. I just had soap and some shower gel, and I needed to wash my uniform. I was looking at my machine gun that I'd left in the kitchen and had the feeling of being alone, very alone.

I felt that that ache in my chest again. I was in love with a woman that I was never going to see. I was very young and all my dreams were disappearing. I had mixed emotions – feeling helpless, useless, little. I wanted something I couldn't have – love. I'd always dreamt about love, but instead I got a love that had been taken away from me. Then I had to go to war. I started to hate everything about myself.

I cleaned myself up and looked around, thinking to myself that I needed to see my grandfather. He lived with his wife, Rose, across the street. I passed many cars that had been destroyed, including my grandfather's. It looked like Swiss cheese – shrapnel holes everywhere but the interior. Fortunately the engine had not been touched.

I walked up to level two and knocked, but nobody answered. I went downstairs to the basement where people had been staying in cramped conditions for several nights. There I found my grandfather and grandmother – well, I called her my grandmother. Rose was a very kind woman.

I tried to describe my first day in the war. My grandfather was not happy or proud. He was a young communist, a proletariat. I mean, he was the guy who was supposed to be a priest, but partisans come into the monastery and recruited him from an early age to be a fighter.

While I was talking to Rose and my grandfather, I saw his eyes were full of tears, but he didn't cry. He was just smoking, and I said to him, "What is it?"

Rose told me, "We don't have insulin anymore, we can't go to the doctor and we can't go to the chemist." I told them I would sort it out, and that the field hospital would have some.

The hospital was only a few kilometres away, so I ran there. I asked the doctor and he gave me enough for thirty days, but said this was the very last supply that they had.

As I was rushing back, the shelling started.

I was running, ducking and lying on the ground. I felt that one of the next shells was going to hit in front, behind or on top of me. My adrenaline kicked in – I felt like I was flying and the fastest guy in the world. Clearly, I was not – I was chubby even then. I got back to the basement in forty minutes and gave my grandfather the insulin.

He couldn't believe it. He said, "All my kids, including your mother, abandoned me. My grandchildren abandoned me – but one grandchild is here to help." I told him life was unpredictable. He was my teacher and mentor. My grandfather was crying because his children had left without telling him, and I was the one who was caring for him.

It was not easy for me to care for him. Everyone knew he was a high-ranking police officer in the communist system. The majority of people did support him as they knew he was good man who had done a lot of good things. Of course, some people in positions of power didn't like that my grandfather was around.

My grandfather gave me some money and told me to go and buy something to eat. I left and set out into the night. All the lights were switched off, and there were no cars and no sound. There was a creepy silence surrounding everything.

I knew most of the people spent the night in makeshift shelters in the basements. I went back upstairs to my apartment and fell asleep, believing I was a hero. Really I was nothing, just a lonely boy who was very lost. My nineteenth birthday was approaching and I knew I wouldn't be celebrating it with my parents. They didn't believe in birthdays and Christmases anyway. I simply thought that one day everything was going to work out well for me.

You wake up in a city that has been under siege from the north, east and south for two months… and yet there are still people walking around and travelling on public transport, trying to function. People were cleaning the rubble, glass, bricks and other debris from the street. I kept wondering how morale remained high and how people were defiant against all the odds. No one knew when the next bombardment was going to start, and there were no signs or warnings that death could be around the corner. There was nobody knocking on the door to tell you the shelling was about to start, to go and hide. People were still walking around, trying to buy things and pay bills.

September 1991 was approaching. The following month, I was going to experience some of the hardest battles back-to-back that would last until the end of November.

In the meantime, I went for some crash courses on being a sniper, a commando, and how to handle landmines and anti-tank combat. They were all short courses – there wasn't the time to train properly. Imagine being a teenager and learning all these skills that were designed for one purpose – to kill others.

My city was being starved to the death. There was only one road in and out, and railroad tracks were sporadic and always targeted. The Federal Army would be receiving reports from the Air Force, who circled above like vultures. We did offer some resistance, with our courage and morale boosted by the desire to be free. We even shot at the planes with everything from pistols to anti-aircraft cannons. I was still in the same summer uniform.

September is officially the start of autumn and with it comes the rain, fog and frost, exactly in that order. That autumn was going to bring more destruction and death than I ever thought possible, with more misery and sadness, and violence escalating on an unimaginable scale.

I already had two months' combat experience behind me. I'd shared this with all different kinds of people from every part of Croatia. Everyone had bled with their focus on independence and democracy, and were determined that we must win every battle.

Every country prepares itself for war. Croatia didn't have that luxury. It was a young country who stood up and started defending their country from an aggressor – an aggressor with the third most powerful army in Europe. This army had invested almost forty-five years in training, equipment, weaponry and tactics, and had allies everywhere around the world. Then there was us – young, green, with little training.

The life of the soldier is very lonely. There is no big mystery to it. You share in the good and the bad with your fellow soldiers, officers and commanders. You even share the bullets. But when the moment comes, as I experienced, every soldier is lonely once they disconnect from their everyday lives. There was a heavy atmosphere hanging over every soldier's head. It stemmed from anxiety, memories of past times with family, friends, husbands, wives and children. Each one of us was fighting the war – not against the enemy in front of you, with their tanks and planes, but a war against yourself. In life, you don't know what your limits are. No one does.

Experts will talk about the fact that you need to think positively. I believe that's partially correct but, when you are on own, it is all about your thoughts and imagination. Something every soldier lives with when he goes into combat is that he has memories of the past. The present only has danger, requiring skills to survive the next attack and the next shelling. In my case, my head was full of my ex-girlfriend and my parents. You don't know what's going to happen next. In those brief moments when you can relax, you find yourself fighting a war against yourself in your head. Nobody can help you – nobody.

I saw many of my comrades start to drink and do other stuff (I had no idea where it came from) to help them numb their minds. You didn't want to think about the next day, with buildings crumbling brick by brick in front of your eyes. Even thinking about what life would be like if you were in another country far away… it all added to the misery and pain.

I came to realise that, regardless of how difficult things got, humans are amazing at improvising. This is especially true in war – when we needed to fix our equipment, lacked ammunition and struggled to find food and water. It can be similar in business – when it feels like you are trapped in a corner, you have no choice but to improvise. Your survival can be down to your next move. When you have taken small steps forward and then are forced to retreat, it is harder to go forward the next time. When you first lose ground, it is always much harder to regain the same ground.

We became known as the Fire Brigade Unit and were awarded a special yellow skull and lightning bolt insignia. The 'Fire Brigade Unit' was an unofficial term – we were a specialist unit of the Ministry of the Interior, sent to 'extinguish fires' here and there.

We were basically pieces of meat who displayed courage and discipline, terrorised the enemy, died with dignity and glorified the political party. We were being sent from one combat to another, filling any gaps. My entire unit was truly fearless. This came from most of them not having children or families. You were dedicated to the cause, but the war in your head was relentless. No one can prepare you for how this feels, so you have to hone your skills, improvise and hope for the best.

We spent a lot of time joking about people's lives and making fun of each other. Some people were a little angry, but we always gave each other hope. Whether I was in combat or at home relaxing, I needed hope to keep me going for another day.

Sometimes your mind would play tricks on you. At night you can smell fear, anxiety and pending violence. I can't explain it, but there is something about the way nature feels around a war zone. When I was on guard duty at night, sometimes it felt like the trees were moving towards you. With the absence of night vision equipment, grass can look like enemy soldiers. In those moments, I often started talking to myself in my head and would look above me at the stars, remembering things from my past. I knew that if I kept looking at the tree in the field in front of me, standing between my village and where the enemy was, I would go crazy. Sure enough, the next day, the tree was still there in the exact same place.

No Candles on My Birthday Cake

"September 1991 marked the beginning of the biggest misery I've everexperienced."

As we approached my birthday in September, I wondered why I should celebrate my birthday. After all, I'd never really done so before. I couldn't care less. I had forgotten I was lonely and my parents hadn't tried to get in touch, not once.

I remembered my very last birthday party had been when I was still at primary school. I was in grade six or seven (in Croatia, primary school goes til year eight). My parents told me I could bring my friends to the house. I arranged for everyone to come at 4pm sharp. At 3:30pm my mum was still sleeping, as she was drunk. I asked her to make some sandwiches for my friends. She said she didn't have any money to buy ham, cheese and bread. That was the last birthday I remember.

September is a beautiful month. The leaves are green or slowly becoming yellow and dark orange. The clouds become heavier and the sun goes down beyond the horizon earlier. Autumn has a smell about it at home, one that I have always liked.

When summer ends, school begins with its new words and new problems. For me, September 1991 marked the beginning of the biggest misery I've ever experienced.

In early September, we were continuously being called upon to go to different battles. One morning around seven o'clock, I received a call to immediately report to the unit and that we were going to be absent for a few days. I expected it to be two or three days, which was what we usually did. Typically, we would get a couple of days to recuperate and then we were off again somewhere else.

However, that day we drove in the truck towards Ernestinovo, where I had spent my first day at war. There was a different feeling in the village now. That morning, Ernestinovo had been bombarded continuously. We heard there was hand to hand combat on the edges of the village. We'd been quickly rushed in and sent to two sectors. We took up our position opposite the church. There was a train station nearby and a tank rolling down the street.

It was an unbelievable scene, and the sheer numbers of infantry soldiers and armoured vehicles surrounding around the village was hard to comprehend. Amazingly, there was no fear or panic.

We were going to fight the enemy again and again. As long as we held ground, we would be okay. Usually their tactics were to start with a short bombardment, with tanks and armoured vehicles, followed with infantry, before finally withdrawing. But that day was different – there were more armoured vehicles, more tanks and more infantry. Combat had been going on for a few hours before we arrived.

I moved from house to house through the walls that had been taken down, so we didn't have to go out into the streets. It was more like a series of tunnels and caves than neighbouring homes.

Combat lasted for some time, and then we were withdrawn towards the village centre. We were exhausted. You could smell the gunpowder on your sweat and there was blood everywhere. Everyone was injured in some way. The bruises and broken fingers were terrible.

Our dedication to the cause was absolute and now was our time to shine. It was hand to hand combat, which we knew was our forté.

The centre of the village was a mix of all these uniforms with different insignia. We went into a small convenience store as we were so incredibly thirsty.

Another group appeared in the store. As we were drinking, we started chatting to each other. Then one of my group recognised a guy in the other group and asked him how he was. I knew him from before, too. He was from my suburb, but had not been with us from the very first day. I knew he wasn't in the city when the war broke out.

In that brief moment, when he started shaking hands with my comrades, the insignia on his left shoulder jumped out at me. It was a group of the enemy Special Forces.

Time just stopped. Imagine a small convenience store, maybe twenty-five square metres. There were about fifteen of us and it was chaotic. We had stopped to have a little break and something to drink. The other group entered and you presumed you were talking to fellow countrymen. Instead, they were enemy soldiers.

In that split second, when everybody turned on each other, all hell broke loose. We were fighting with hands, bottles, knives and guns. We decided to get the fuck out of this place. My group were out, trying to circle the store and force the enemy to surrender. They were trying to do the same thing.

It was the most horrifying experience I'd had. In that small, confined space, it was truly a fight for life between us. It was not like the movies – no special moves, no machine guns. It was purely bottles, knives and attempts to reach for guns to try and shoot.

The day was coming to an end. Fights were slowly dying down, with just a few skirmishes continuing. It had been a hell of a day on both sides. I'd truly believed that my life was going to end that day. I was shooting, running and looking for cover all day. I shot 7,000 bullets. And I cried, I really cried that day.

When the fight ended, we eventually took up positions in a big, white house on the intersection of two streets. It was a beautiful house and by some miracle it was still intact. I was sitting on the stairs of the porch with my machine gun, covered in soot. I knew that I needed to clean my gun as I was going to need it again soon.

I asked my aide to find a suitable position where we could look over the field towards the enemy village. He went inside and smashed a couple bricks in the bathroom to make an opening for me.

I was slowly cleaning my gun, crying as I did so. I was afraid. I knew I had certainly dodged death that day. Being so close to dying was a terrifying experience – even more so as it was not by bullets, but with hands, bottles and knives. Is this what my life had come to?

Something else was forming that day – leadership. We had commanding officers who didn't walk around parading. They were checking in with everybody. "Here's some ammunition. How do you feel? Are you wounded?"

Leadership was taking care of everybody. Leadership was being built by taking responsibility and accountability for every soul under your command. I was impressed with my commanding officers. Their first thought was to care for us – not to take their boots off and shout outorders to bring them water, food and other things. They checked in with everyone.

They got us to form a huddle to discuss where we were, what we needed, what the best extraction point was, what to expect and what we could see in front of us. We need to run 1.5km to the waterfall to bring buckets of water to drink. Nobody wanted to go back to the middle of the village, which had been smashed with all the shelling and shooting – but we did. Tanks and armoured vehicles were running through the homes, crushing everything in front of them.

I wasn't the only one who had been crying. I was shaking with the cold, too. There were enemy soldiers a few metres away. We were shooting them from only thirty to fifty metres away. It was slaughter. Heavy shelling was coming from every possible direction. You didn't know who was shelling who. We couldn't get out until there was support, as the enemy was so close.

I stopped crying and told my commanding officer I was going upstairs to sit for a while. I needed a rest from carrying the weight of my machine gun. It was a big, heavy boy. After using it, you just want to wash your hands and face, sit down and have a smoke.

We knew it was not over and that they were going to come back – maybe not that afternoon, but the next day. They had tasted victory and knew that they could break us. We also knew that we could be broken. We had weapons but couldn't match the numbers. The numbers were against us.

Kids are Safe, But Parents are Hanging in the Closet

"My dad is a police officer. My mum says she can't live like this anymore. She is very, very sad. My daddy doesn't want to leave."

We walked back into the big, white house. It looked like a perfect target, but for some reason it was the only house that had not been shot at. Something deep inside me felt that this house wasn't going to last much longer. It was only later that we realised it was being used as a marker, or lighthouse if you will, to line ammunition up against us.

I walked upstairs into a pristine bedroom with a large bed, white sheets and pillows. I couldn't believe how impeccably clean it was. Even the sheets still smelt nice, like they had been washed a few days earlier. The window was open, with the curtains dancing in the window. You'd have thought nothing out of the ordinary was going on around the house.

I sat on the edge of the bed, wondering if it would be okay to lie down and dirty the clean sheets from my grubby uniform. There was a wardrobe facing the bed and a picture of a husband and wife on the bedside table. *Where were these people?* I thought. Did they know we were in their home, making a stand against an army? The picture next to it was of the couple with their two daughters. I remember thinking there was a big age difference between the girls.

Then my aide came in and offered me a coffee. We chatted briefly, then I said I wanted to crash and asked him to come and get me in ten minutes.

I looked at myself in the mirror – all covered in black dust – then lay down and fell asleep. I dreamt of making love; it was so beautiful. A few bullets ricocheted off the house and woke me up.

The coffee was still warm, so I sat on the edge of the bed and drank it, trying to come to my senses, trying to be brave. I told myself, "You know why you are here. Be the man. You can do it."

I looked down and, to my amazement, saw a book I remembered from primary school. The daughter must have brought it in here to show her parents. It put a smile on my face. They must have left in a hurry. I started reading the stories and notes the girl had written in the margins of the book and the memories came back to me.

Coming to the end of the book I noticed a lot of blank pages. School must have stopped due to the war and nothing was written in May and June.

On the last page she wrote, *"My dad is a police officer. My mum says she can't live like this anymore. She is very, very sad. My daddy doesn't want to leave."* So it was the house of a police officer from the communist system. I put the book down next to my coffee cup.

The wardrobe was ajar and for some reason I decided to open it slowly. The door squeaked. The husband and wife were hanging inside.

I took a deep breath. I grabbed a blanket, lay them down on the floor and covered them, before saying a quick prayer.

I started looking in the other rooms for the girls. I found their rooms, which were almost empty. There were few clothes or books. They must have gone and for some reason decided to come back. Maybe they didn't want to leave the home. I have no idea.

'Till death do us part' was literal for this poor couple.

Surrounded

"That feeling when you see dust falling from the ceilings, glass shaking on the floor."

Laslovo was surrounded 90% and we didn't have the same reserves or equipment as a normal army. It seemed unfathomable to me that while I was outside my city fighting in the war, life in my city was somehow continuing on as per usual.

Summer heat makes you extra thirsty. No matter how much water you drank, your throat would be burning and even grass feels like a knife cutting you. Water was a commodity. Every house had underground water and a pump in their front or back yard – but reaching that house to fill your canisters would be like playing Russian roulette. You were in constant danger of being caught by enemy snipers – so you'd use every skill to stay invisible when fetching water. Sometimes I couldn't care less if the sniper hit me. Moments like these are when you battle yourself inside your head – and the only thing that could bring me back to reality was a call over radio from some of my boys, who noticed how reckless I'd become. I wasn't the only one.

There was a moment when I was sent to bring water, because I was the youngest, with a few of the other boys. Suddenly we heard that terrifying *click-clack* of metal caterpillars on hot asphalt, and the occasional shooting with automatic rifles. The sound grew closer and closer. Screw the water – we ran into a nearby house, a position which was given to us earlier.

The beautifully-built house had two floors and was filled with new furniture and dust, windows with broken glass. I always wondered who the people were who were living in this house, what they looked like and what they did for a living. I had so many questions and only my imagination could answer based on few pieces of life that family had left behind.

Our position was on the first floor, with a few guys below us on the ground floor. We got the order to wait for the enemy to come closer, as we knew that as soon as the armour entered the urban area, all we needed to deal was the infantry. It is easier to say than to do, but we had no choice – except to fight to live or surrender and die. At least I was perceiving situations like that.

That feeling when you see dust falling from the ceilings, glass shaking on the floor. The look in our eyes was horrific, mixed fear and excitement. So many things were flying around in front of our eyes. I wished I was somewhere else enjoying a cold drink.

Late summer afternoon in the village, a shadow passed overhead where minutes were like hours and hours were like years. You pray that time passes quickly and you return to the safety of your own city.

The earth was trembling and sporadic shooting became more intense. The troopers behind us started shooting, with a few mortar explosions in the middle of the village.

I caught a glimpse of some of my boys in the house opposite me, hiding behind gates and preparing an RPG (rocket launcher M-57) as they were preparing to hit the first vehicle. It was primitive but powerful on close proximity to the armour. In practice we should hit the last vehicle as well, so all the other armoured vehicles would stay trapped without being able to move. We could then pick them off one by one as long as the infantry had been dealt with.

In next few moments a rocket exploded on an armoured personnel vehicle. That is all what I saw – but it was what I saw next that made me realise we were all going to die. Behind the armoured vehicle was a tank, which was parked in front our house. The barrel was lifting up and up. I was silent – and then the next moment the explosion came.

The detonation of that explosion sent us flying across the room. All I heard was my boys gasping for air, with dust in our eyes and lungs, our ears and noses bleeding. We were blind.

The experience of that hit felt equal to a nuclear explosion we'd seen in documentaries. We were searching for each other by calling out our names. Then I felt my weapon under my finger, and was crawling toward window for more air – while someone in my group told me, *"Stay down. Don't do this."* I needed air, though, and so I saw the barrel of the tank aiming at the ground floor.

The next explosion lifted us up then we sank to the ground floor. All I could hear from the outside were enemy soldiers who were arguing about whether to throw hand grenades or not. We started shooting at them without stopping – blinded by the light coming from outside. Our training in combat and how to refill clips with munition, how to unjam weapons, was paying off. Suddenly the enemy were fleeing.

It lasted no more than thirty minutes, but I felt it was an eternity. We'd survived with so many scratches and cuts, swallowing so much dust – but we'd defended our position. Simultaneously, I knew if they continued to attack us stronger than this each time, we would eventually suffer defeat. At this moment, though, to me I felt like the biggest hero – and we shared some drinks, water and food while holding positions til the next day, when our replacements were coming.

The dust had settled, the fires had extinguished and we could see the house again. Somehow, we were left to live another day. All I wanted was to share my story with everyone – you know, like you see in the movies, where the heroes survive all odds while the audience holds their breath – yet I didn't have anyone to share it with. Somehow, I felt that the world didn't care.

The following day, I was back home with the team and finally went for that cold drink in the city. On TV, a journalist was explaining what happened in that village and I felt silent – knowing this is just beginning of the hell ahead of me. It was the summer I wished everything was different.

Let Me Sleep, Please

"Somehow, people found a way to supply bread and milk, open shops and clean the streets every day."

The normally beautiful month of September had a difficult start. We were rushing from one side of the country to the other, fighting so many battles, travelling from one front line and village to another. It was endless, September was endless – yet it seemed that the enemy were trying to bring an end to the fighting.

There was an oil refinery on the outskirts of my city. They had never fired on it until the third of September, just before my birthday. They pounded it all day and finally smashed the refinery. The flames were visible for days. When firemen tried to extinguish the fire, they would be shot at. It was a very effective way to demoralise the civilians. The thick smoke looked like a black cross above the city.

We were exhausted. The entire country was exhausted, but the willpower for freedom and democracy remained. We had also started to get some new equipment, uniforms and weapons – but unfortunately still no heavy equipment, tanks, armoured vehicles or planes. Nothing.

We could feel that something was changing. The behaviour of the enemy was becoming more aggressive and more violent, if that was possible. Bombardments would start in the morning, continue for a few hours, then restart again and continue late into the night. Sometimes it would start as early as four or five o'clock. Psychologically, it was devastating. Even on my days off, I would sleep in the basement, surrounded by civilians and hugging my weapon.

Every time a grenade fell you would hear a scream, broken glass and then silence – every time. There was a kind of vacuum in the air, with all the mortars and grenades raining down. I was always on high alert, in a state of readiness. The bombardments became excruciating.

I hardly got any time at home in September. The fighting went on day after day, night after night. We knew we had problems. Our lines were holding, but there was simply not enough manpower or weaponry to properly defend them. The disruption to transport and logistics from the continuous bombardment was immense.

Somehow, people found a way to supply bread and milk, open their shops and clean the streets every day. I could see how the villages and my city were being reduced to rubble. There were papers and pictures blown all over the street, memories of families literally flying out the windows as each grenade hit. It was a horrific sight. September, my birthday month, had become a series of terrifying experiences. There were fewer civilians around the city.

Meanwhile Vukovar, in the far east of Croatia, was under siege. It was surrounded, with just one road in that was being slowly closed down.

The enemy started using different tactics, with more and more paramilitary units coming across into Croatia. They attacked mercilessly. I wondered how long we were going to be able to withstand this. I knew we were being driven from one position to another. Everyone was under enormous pressure, regardless of how much effort we put in.

October was the month that it would start to get cold, and the first real rain would fall. Golden September became grey, sombre October. It was only a question of time before snow would appear and winter would start. As a kid, I remember enjoying chestnuts on the fire. You could buy them on every street corner and enjoy walking home with black fingers from the charred chestnuts.

I was sleeping in my unit on an unusually quiet day. The rain was pouring down and everything was soaked. A handful of cars and busses passed by. I was lucky that my grandparents had cooked and cleaned for me.

As I lay in bed, my mind wandered. I just wanted to be hugged and feel the warmth of a woman next to me. I wished someone would tell me to wake up and that it was just a dream.

I still hadn't heard from my parents. They had been in touch with my grandfather, though – so I knew they were in my father's home village with my brother. Basically they'd only been in touch as they needed to report to the factory once a week so that they'd get paid. They forgot to do it, so they needed me to beg officials to record them as if they were coming. Hence they got paid, and I got nothing.

It was four months into the war. I was losing my hair and my face had become different. There was rarely a smile there anymore. I had become a very different person. I was a young adult, not a teenager, and I had become very serious. I had even started enjoying vodka! Despite my doubts and miseries, I had become a war junkie who relished causing pain to the enemy, the feeling of action and the adrenaline surging through my body.

The friends I had been hanging out with just a few months ago were now spread far and wide. I was in a company of grown-up men who had their own challenges from not seeing their children, families or partners. I was sort of okay, because I didn't have anybody.

Then there was a knock on my door. I was dressed and opened the door to the mailman. It struck me how amazing it was that mail kept being delivered through the war. He gave me a letter with a look of hatred in his eyes. He didn't know I was a soldier; I was just dressed in a tracksuit. I didn't understand that look. He just said, "Letter for you."

The mailman was usually was a very kind man, but that day he wasn't. He gave me the letter and turned his back.

I looked to see the letter was addressed to me with a female's handwriting and an address from Belgrade, Serbia on the back. It had my girlfriend's name on it. I hadn't spoken to her for the past four months and I was in shock. That one letter changed my entire behaviour.

I slowly opened the letter and made a coffee. It was a couple of A4 pages long and she was explaining where she was, what she was doing, how her family was and even what was cool. Then, right at the end, she told me she hated me and I was at war with her. She had also found a man.

I was very sad and upset. *"Oh, God. Why? Why this letter now?"*

I kept that letter in my pocket. Every time I had a chance, I would reread it. She had reached me to tell me that she slept with somebody else. I wasn't at war with her. For a brief moment, it made me feel my life was over. It wasn't over, though. Of course it wasn't over.

I tried to understand why somebody would want add more misery to your life by showing you how happy they were. I have witnessed this so many times. People love to stick it to your face, poke you in the eye and shout loudly that they are happier than you.

I replied to her, simply saying that I would always love her and that I hoped she was okay. I added that I truly believed that one day we were going to meet again, or at least talk. I sent that letter without hate for all the things she had told me.

That was the beginning of my October – rain and more fuel on the fire of my broken heart. There was no extinguisher by my side, nobody around to help me to understand why I loved her so much.

Curing the Pneumonia with Grappa

The doctor said, "Take it easy for a few days and snort some grappa."

The smell of late summer was replaced by October's rainy days. I was lucky enough to attend a couple of Croatian courses on a psychological warfare. Nobody wanted to do it, but I did. I wanted to learn more, I wanted to understand what was happening around me.

I tried to understand all the propaganda that the enemy was forcing on us daily. When I had some down time, I would often lie on my bed and watch TV. The horror of the war in Croatia was constantly talked about, with the successes of the Croatian Army and police being constantly promoted.

Then I would change channels to Serbian TV. The shows were the same, but they talked about how terrible we were and how we were a cruel army hurting civilians, which was not true. Other channels still showed parties and happy daytime talk shows. Of course, after midnight, there was porn. Well, porn doesn't know the borders or the sides of war.

That's how I would usually fall asleep, until I woke up to someone calling me to find out whether I was ready for my next assignment.

In October, I contracted pneumonia. I was coughing blood for days and couldn't breathe properly through my nose. The doctor told me there was no medicine available, apart from some paracetamol and something for my temperature.

They couldn't even do x-rays. He just listened to my lungs and he told me, "Take it easy for a few days and snort some grappa." Yes, snort, rather than drink, grappa. He said it was 40% alcohol and snorting it, along with paracetamol, would have me right in twenty-four hours.

Well, I wasn't okay in twenty-four hours. It took me two or three days before my bleeding stopped. I still went to the front line where I'd be snorting grappa. No one said anything – it was some kind of traditional medicine our grandparents used one hundred years ago. I used my father's grappa, the same stuff he would drink in the morning and salute himself with. If I couldn't get grappa, I used vodka. Finally, the pneumonia started going away. I felt rejuvenated when I wasn't bleeding anymore.

My whole unit was sharing the same destiny. Everybody had some kind of disease, mainly because we went into winter in the same uniforms we had for the height of summer. I tried to find some jumpers, something with long sleeves I could tuck in under my uniform. I looked more like a clown than a soldier, but those were the times.

You could be prepared physically and even spiritually, but mentally I was breaking down. There were breaking points on a daily basis. I just wanted to sleep and wake up in the morning to find everything was over. From a physical perspective, I was getting blisters on my feet every day. You would pierce them, put on a bandage and start marching.

That's how I went into November. The military situation across Croatia was very bleak and it did not look like we were going to win the war, yet everybody was giving it their all. It was a bit like a meat machine on both sides. We didn't have a reserve army or troops to replace people on the front line, so we kept being rushed from one point to another.

The first snow started falling gently. I was standing on a street, waiting for the transport to come pick me up. I felt all these snowflakes falling on my face. It made me feel like a kid again.

I used to look forward to winter for the snow. As a child, the buses would be going slowly through the snow, so we would hold on to the back of the bus and be pulled skiing on our feet behind them.

It was becoming very cold. The frost made the soil very hard to walk on. The metal parts of your weapon would stick, so you were constantly cleaning to keep them warm and ready. We were all still in our summer uniforms.

The Cornfields

"Obviously this was the place where I was going to die."

We were sitting in the back of a truck in November with a cold, frosty wind coming from all directions. I recognised the road. I knew we were heading back towards the village of Ernestinovo, where I had fought my first day. This time we went to a different position, securing the route between the villages that the enemy could intercept and cut off at any moment.

We would try to make jokes. Some guys would talk about having sex with their wives or girlfriends. I was told often, "Mario, you are getting old, you're changing and losing your hair." I knew my life was different and that I was undergoing something of a metamorphosis.

Almost five months into the war, I was just barely nineteen years old. Apart from having my MG42, I got a knife as I knew sooner or later I was going to be in a position where I couldn't carry that weapon, had no ammunition and was surrounded. I needed something for personal defence. I didn't want to take a gun – that was too fancy for me and I didn't believe in small calibres.

You could see the city was becoming a ghost town. The first snow was sticking to the soil and the trees had lost their leaves. There were no cars on the street, just the check points.

There was danger everywhere across Croatia. We were tired, and the enemy had a pool of reserve soldiers and volunteers. We only had us and we knew it. It was just a question of when some of the lines would be broken. We were thinly spread, but wherever we were one thing was certain: we would not let anyone pass us and fight until our last drop of the blood.

We had our special insignia, but still no winter uniforms. We had ammunition, but no new weapons. We had food, but it dated from the 1950s and 60s. There was no more cooked food.

The truck stopped on the road with open fields either side. The enemy villages were a few kilometres away. They could see us, but we couldn't see them.

We arrived at a motel and I was remembering how, just a few months ago, this place was being visited by many people. There would have been live music, drinking, food and enjoyment. It was a 'naked' motel. Naked means no doors, windows or furniture, nothing. I didn't hear my orders, as I couldn't care less anymore. I went looking for my position.

I walked inside with a few of my boys. Our senior officer was talking to my commanding officer, telling us we needed to stay here for the next forty-eight hours. The intelligence services had information that the enemy was about to move hard over this area. If they broke this line, the next four or five villages would fall. They would come straight to my city. There were thirty-five kilometres of open fields, perfect for their armoured vehicles. Obviously, this was the place where I was going to die.

It was very quiet. We were looking for where we were going to sit and lie down. They found a big bed from one of the rooms. It had no mattress or anything.

We were cold and lit a fire inside. There was a stink of ham that came from the canned food. We'd worked out how to bake food inside the cans. Yeah, it was a little bit of a laugh as we shared the little bit of grub we had. Then I started coughing again, followed by someone else and someone else. Half of us were very sick and running a temperature. I saw blood again in my palm. I said to myself, "Not again." Then you wonder to yourself, *"What else I can endure? What else can control me?"*

I was going to use the grappa and snort a couple of paracetamols. Some guys had different types of medicines and offered them to me, but I said no. I knew deep inside of me that this was just another day, and just another drop of my blood from my lungs into my palm. This is just part of life. *I can do it. I can survive.* How mistaken I was.

From military point of view, I could understand the importance of this position between two villages connected by flat roads. There was maybe three kilometres between Ernestinovo and Laslovo. They needed to protect that route, and there was the possibility to outflank and cut off the enemy. There were only three or four of us, no more. From a logistical point of view, it was a nightmare. If you have any wounded, it can easily be seen by the enemy from all sides when the trucks or a vehicle tries to come and collect them. You had to expect shelling, snipers and any type of weapon possible that could be used to destroy communication between that motel and the villages on both sides.

We had terrible night vision, and didn't know who could come during the night. Even our vehicles were hard to recognise when driving without lights to bring us food or other supplies.

A lot happened that night. The sun had set and gone. This usually happened around 4pm and it became very cold very quickly. It wasn't just the frost – the temperature dropped to one or two degrees below zero, maybe more.

Everything was freezing, including the paddocks on the road. The water and the rations would be next – but we knew that we needed to put out our fire, as in the night you could see it from a kilometre away. Just imagine the motel, in the middle of the road, surrounded by open fields, with a fire inside. That was when they liked to shoot at us, so we needed to extinguish the fire.

I was leaning next to the window, seeing what was happening in front of the motel. Everybody was at the one window, looking around. We had two guards outside, but that was it. We did not have enough men to cover one motel. It was more like a D-Day bunker on the Normandy beaches. Light was getting dimmer and there was a very soft speaking radio on minimum volume. Apart from that, there was silence.

I was watching the sky grow darker and darker. Stars in the sky became brighter and brighter. Your eyes are wide open, soaking in every possible light, scanning the environment, because the last thing that you needed was something to call on your enemies. Suppose you accidently fired at the trees or threw a hand grenade. That would be it for us.

Then you get up. Living this life, you get up with the desire to leave. You don't care anymore that you're sick with a temperature and you're coughing blood. You have your jacket, equipment and weapons always at the ready, the trigger finger ready to shoot.

You're not tired, you're not thirsty. And the stars are so bright, like you have put a Christmas tree in the sky.

Then the full moon appeared, with its welcoming illumination of the hills around us. Something was amongst all of us. We became very uncomfortable, thinking it was possibly something in our minds. Something odd happened as the night went on.

We had one person observing and guarding the motel, while the others would sleep. I remember four of us squeezed together like sardines on that king-sized bed. There was no mattress, no pillows – nothing. We were lying down, with all our equipment and in our uniforms, holding each other, trying to keep warm. One of the boys found some old curtains to cover us. The curtains were full of holes.

Then my shift came from 3am to 5am. Honestly, I hated those shifts. I knew my body just wanted to sleep and was shutting down. I knew I had to push myself to stay awake. Even though the purpose of everything was to preserve your life and defend your country, your body had a different idea, trying to find ways to slow you down. You had to try and fight your biological clock. You try to push yourself, imagine having a coffee or talking to somebody in your head.

I listened to what was happening outside. Your eyes and ears become your best friend, along with your nose. I saw the first light on horizon slowly appearing, and I knew I'd survived another day. Maybe it was ridiculous to think that way, but I believed that seeing the first light was the way to count my days of surviving another night. Now I could go home, cough up blood and it was going to be okay.

One of my comrades came to ask how I was. I just said to him, "Can you hear that?" I swore to God I could hear something moving through the cornfields.

He says, "Mario, you're imagining things."

"Listen and look at the window," I said. He checked one of our comrades' watches with his torch, checking the time. It was 4:45 in the morning. I said, "I'm going to go wake up the others."

Then I realised what I'd heard. It was not my imagination. In the cornfield, slowly but certainly, the plants were breaking and the grass was moving.

Everybody was awake in the next two or three minutes. Everybody was at the windows. As the light was appearing, the sound disappeared. Then, it appeared again and disappeared. The tension in us was so high.

Then we got a call on the radio. An observer in one of the villages could see a large group of enemy soldiers, surrounding us from all sides. All night, they'd seen saw sporadic lights in the fields and in the forest and followed us.

I asked my comrade what the time was, to which he said it was 5am.

I replied, "Well, if something is going to happen, it would happen now."

He looked at me and said, "Maybe it's just a false alarm. Maybe everybody is imagining things." We started laughing.

That very moment an RPG hit the wall of the room we were in, then a second RPG. I remember I went flying from my window to the middle of the room. Everything was suddenly so dusty – with dust in my eyes, nose and mouth. Then the gunfire exchanges started.

I tried to rush to my position to man my weapon, but I couldn't move my left arm because I had dislocated my shoulder from the ferocity of the explosion in the wall. I couldn't move my left arm, but yet I told myself, "Mario you must do this." I ignored the pain, lifted my left arm, walked to my machine gun and started shooting.

One of the soldiers ran from ground floor upstairs and said, "Infantry is coming from all sides. Some of them have RPGs." He could see some M60 mortars, the perfect weapon for infantry charges. Due to the lights from all the explosions, he couldn't see how many of them there were behind the mortar positions, a couple of hundred metres away.

I knew it, we all knew it. We going to now experience something that we didn't want – being surrounded on all sides.

The clash started. The ferocity of the attack was extreme. The bullets were flying through the windows from all directions, with mortars, RPGs and 64 millimetre rocket launchers. It was explosion after explosion, so many that I couldn't hear anymore. We were screaming inside, but we knew we couldn't surrender. We knew we should, but our destiny would be totally different. We were all going to fight and die together.

I was manning my machine gun when I saw them – infantry against infantry in an open field. They were running like crazy, like something from the medieval age. I was not sure what was going to happen.

Then something outrageous happened. For some reason, the attack stopped, like nothing had happened. I saw, in the distance, a couple of armoured personnel vehicles who had come to help us. They started shooting. They were anti-aircraft vehicles, mounted with three 20 millimetre cannons. They were levelling the horizon and they helped us so much.

The Water Pump

*"Surrender. Don't leave your bones here.
We're going to look after you."*

After this attack, I temporarily lost my hearing. At the time I didn't know whether I'd lost my hearing forever. There were no doctors who could check this, so there was no testing.

Instead of going home, the commanding officer came to us and said, "You're going to be transferred over to the other side, a kilometre and a half away. It's a water pump station. You need to replace the crew. They're being massacred there. They've lost munitions, they've lost a couple members of the unit. They're in very bad shape."

In ten to fifteen minutes, we replenished our food, munitions and everything. As we went, we shared the smokes amongst each other. Somebody had coffee in a thermos. We drank it like it was water.

We started marching and crawling, walking and ducking, a kilometre and a half through the frozen land until we finally reached the water pump station. We replaced the crew – some of them stayed with us. They told us they'd been simultaneously hit with tanks and everything because they were so close to the enemy village.

By midday, we knew that we were going to feel tenfold what we had felt the day before. We were so isolated. On one side there was the forest, while on the other side and behind us there were open fields. On both sides there were also enemy villages teeming with the soldiers, equipment and tanks that we could clearly hear.

They were driving around. Then, for the very first time, I heard the speakers. Somebody, presumably a commanding officer, was screaming, "Surrender. Don't leave your bones here. We're going to look after you."

We just looked at each other and laughed. But essentially what they were saying to us was, *"That was a sign. Look what's coming. It will be much, much worse, much more intense, with much more wallop than the day before in the motel."*

We took our position in that water pump station. It was a horrific sight, a bit like a scene from a horror movie – with the walls of the station covered with bloodstains and bullet holes. It was hard to believe how isolated we were from the main body of the Army.

It was the worst location imaginable in terms of the ability to escape. There was no real possibility of extraction. However, with its thick concrete walls the water pump station was a perfect place to defend, and the enemy didn't know how many of us were there. The best part was that it was situated on a little hill with a lot of concrete places you could hide in. It was like a ready-made bunker.

The days spent in that station were very pleasant by comparison, as we could finally recuperate ourselves. This was despite the fact we had psychological warfare impacting us for the very first time. Each day, all day, they were calling for us to surrender. Then afterwards we'd wonder why they were calling for us to surrender. There are so many more of them – I would say at least five to one, if not more. They had tanks, mortars, cannons and rocket launchers. Why were they telling us to surrender?

We started telling each other the story that perhaps we had done such a good job at that plush motel that they had experienced much higher losses than they'd anticipated. We also started telling each other that their morale must be low, as ours was sky high. We didn't feel cold, tired or hungry. We didn't want to sleep, we just wanted to continue with this. Maybe, subconsciously we wanted to die. Then we'd start talking about our families and the past. There was always some story out there about somebody, and we laughed at the humour of them.

Then reality hit and I was coughing badly. I knew it, I was very sick. My shoulder was hurting like hell. One of my comrades said he would fix my shoulder, but I told him not to touch it as I could barely move. I was carrying my thirteen kilo weapon in one hand, and shared the munition belts with my aide. He told me I had to stand against the wall. He smacked me so hard in my left shoulder I think it dislocated again in different directions.

Amazingly it stopped hurting so much and I had a little bit of vodka. We had one of those small hotel-type bottles between us. We all shared the one little bottle as though we were celebrating at a wedding.

We laughed at this, but deep inside of us we knew that this was the beginning of the end. The enemy was strong in every single direction, and the news we were getting from the completely cut-off city was not pleasant whatsoever. They had been cut off for days now and bombarded 24/7. The news we heard was that the enemy were taking some positions inside the city, but some brave civilians had pushed them out. We wanted to believe in all of this, but the city was full of soft targets like homes, and we knew that they would fall. We felt depressed. We had more and more enemies coming towards us with more and more equipment.

There was no doubt they were having casualties, too, as their way of attack changed. It had been a short artillery barrage, followed immediately by charging tanks and armoured vehicles, with lots of enemies behind them. Then they started having longer bombardments, believing that this was going to force a surrender.

The night was just as cold as the night before. During the day, I had seen frost melting off the leaves and freezing again once it hit the ground. This was yet another night in my summer uniform.

The strikers of war continuously called on us to surrender. Sometime after 10pm they fell silent, so we expected them all night long. We didn't even talk. We didn't drink, we didn't smoke. We just waited. Minutes felt like hours.

We waited more, thinking they were going to repeat the same thing they did the day before. But they didn't come. We heard on the radio that replacements were coming.

Then we saw the tanks coming through the forest. You could hear the trucks, but could only see the barrels of their heavy weapons when they were a few hundred metres away.

Wave after wave charged on us. There was no doubt they were testing our positions. They knew what kind of resistance to expect. I told myself, "I feel sorry for whoever comes after us, because they know we are not going to stop fighting until they have taken our position."

Thankfully, maybe due to the ferociousness of our defence and the number of casualties they suffered, they never fully engaged. Our resistance was always so fierce, so I guess the enemy thought there were more of us than what there were. This sowed fear into them, as we fought to take as many lives as we could and show them we weren't just some kids, show that our resistance was better than their attack.

Later on, we were on a truck back to the city. The villages I had seen days before were even emptier. There were less people, all the gates were barricaded and you could see chains around the gate posts. It meant that people had left their homes.

Finally, when we reached the city, I saw the doctor and told him of my shoulder. He inspected it, told me it was dislocated and that he would fix it. He caused me even more pain and I sat there, still coughing blood. He said he couldn't give me anything, but if I came back in a few hours' time he would find some penicillin and vaccines. He said it was going to help more than the grappa.

The Water Pump

I went home. I was so cold and just felt grey as I moved around very gingerly. The city was becoming wrapped in fog and snow. That was mid-November 1991 and the misery was neverending.

I had deep thoughts, questioning everything, questioning myself. Mentally, I was exhausted and broken. All I wanted was to sleep – but not just to lie down and get sleep. I wanted somebody to hug me and tell me how much they loved me. I wanted to kiss someone and feel the warmth of their skin.

November was a month without much relaxing. There was no time to relax. The military situation in Croatia became very grim and many positions had become impossible to defend. We had less men. Despite the desire of many to fight, the odds were against us. But we did fight. We fought day after day across Croatia, defending our country, defending democracy, defending our livelihoods, our homes, our families and our friends.

The news depicted that the situation was bad. It was a month when the many positions became unattainable, and the faint-hearted became suicidal, while still remaining involved in the war. You felt the full force of the enemy and the technology against you. On a daily basis, you faced thousands of shells raining on your position from airplanes above, shooting in every possible direction. The number of bombs everywhere was just unbelievable.

I was called to join the big task force group to break into the city of Vukovar in the east of Croatia and help the defenders inside. We were to carry military equipment, medical supplies and food. We had no idea how it would work. We just knew we needed to break the blockade, enter the city, bring all the equipment and help the defenders and civilians to leave the city.

The city of Vukovar was looking the way the Battle of Stalingrad did in documentaries on the History Channel – continuous hand-to-hand combat, with ever-weary survivors. When you listen to all the interviews with survivors describing the war, it looked exactly like this. The planes destroyed hundreds of things. It was a slaughter on industrial scale. The enemy had more of everything –

more power, technology, weapons, mechanised equipment, plans, tanks and armoured vehicles. We couldn't match them in this area, but we knew hand-to-hand combat, and we knew that we could beat them in urban warfare, if not on the open fields.

We left the city of Vinkovci around 2 or 3 am in the morning. I remember that I just wanted to talk to my parents and see how they were, to tell them that this was most probably going to be the last time they ever heard from me.

I knew that once when we entered Vukovar, nobody would come out alive. Despite the defensive effort, despite everything, this city was being overwhelmed from all sides. It looked like an impossible task, but the fire was still in me. The desire to fight for my country, for my comrades and for civilians was huge.

Fallen, Broken, Jesus

"The hands of Jesus on the cross were covered in mud and blood, obviously from local civilians or soldiers touching it."

We walked 15km into the village of Nustar on a cold November morning. Everything was frozen around us. The fog was immensely thick. It was like a sign of the horror we were heading into. We walked quietly, carrying all our equipment. As we walked along the road in the fog, we saw other units around us. Heads were held high, but we all knew we were walking towards the city of Vukovar with limited resources.

First, we needed to stop in the village to get our orders. We didn't know what was ahead of us. All we knew was that the situation was bad in every way. The weather was the crappiest weather you could imagine to try and do anything in. The ground was frozen solid, the fog surrounded you and you had open fields around with nowhere to hide, nowhere to escape. We just needed to cross a few kilometres. I love that word – 'just' a few kilometres, 'just' break the blockade, 'just' pierce a hole into the ring of steel around the city, and 'just' enter inside.

As we walked towards the village, the fog became so thick. I couldn't even see anybody in front of me. I could hear steps, but everything else was quiet. From a military perspective, it was a great cover as the enemy couldn't see you walking. As we approached, I was trying to look around to see who was next to me and behind me.

Suddenly, I felt I lost the ground under my feet and started rolling into some type of frozen mud. The equipment was hitting me all over my body and I felt somebody's weapon smacking my face. We all started falling onto each other. Then, just like that, the fog lifted a little. I saw there was an enormous hole than dozens of us had fallen into. It was such a huge crater, at least twenty metres down and thirty metres across.

As we tried to climb out of the pit, I felt it was a bad sign. Then, as I came to the edge of the crater, I saw a cross in front of me. We were in a front of church, with Jesus Christ on the cross, damaged and broken on half, so the cross was facing down towards the ground. I saw the hands of Jesus on the cross were covered in mud and blood, obviously from local civilians or soldiers touching it.

The church was full of holes. As we climbed out of the crater, there was a silence. Nobody was saying anything.

We had a short break and were told to pick up the equipment and march towards the village. As we marched, memories of my life and my childhood started crossing my mind. I couldn't shake the impression of the broken cross facing the ground. Everyone had the feeling it was a bad omen.

Suddenly, the fight started on the edges of the village. After the skirmishes and exchanges of fire ceased, we start moving towards the city of Vukovar.

The fog didn't want to lift. It felt it was like seven o'clock in the morning and the cold air was in your lungs. We were slowly chatting amongst ourselves, being able to see each other more and more clearly as the fog lifted. We had doubts that we were going to come out of the village alive.

Now that we had a local guide to lead us, we'd reached the bank of a small river. Through the fog we saw so many tanks, armoured vehicles and inventory facing towards the village we'd just left. We were already facing the steel ring around the city when the firing started. It became so intense.

After a few hours, we were ordered to retreat back into the village. As we retreated, I saw people hiding in basements, full of fear and going crazy. I think that was the first time I saw somebody have a nervous breakdown because of the shelling, the tanks and everything around us.

I had never seen anything like this, seeing the enemy soldiers so close and in that fog. As we were all slowly retreating back, exchanging fire, we were told that the city had surrendered. We were so sad and broken.

A few days later, my city had been completely surrounded as our troops couldn't defend the villages around the fields or the command posts that had given a breathing space to my city. The enemy closed the gap around us and was conquering the remaining places in Croatia. Our morale sank.

What had been defending the whole country turned into a static war defending the one city, with trenches being dug all around – yes, trenches in the twentieth century. We were digging trenches to defend the city. I felt this is it. This was truly our last stand.

The University

"The enemy had camouflage snow uniforms and they were crawling across the two kilometres of fields."

December 1991 was one of the coldest months I could recall. Just twelve months earlier, the previous December had been some of the most perfect days of my life. I had been in love. I had been in a capital city with my girl. To be surrounded with people in a technologically advanced city, with so much to discover and explore, was wonderful. I remember I often went to church and prayed, thanking God for everything that was happening in my life. I was conscious of things changing around us, but I decided not to believe it. Then they changed forever.

Snow started falling towards the end of November, and in December we finally got our first winter uniforms – camouflage ones with proper boots and socks.

Interestingly enough, I'd never been paid for the previous five months. I didn't have money, I didn't have anything, but I didn't expect anything either. I didn't know any better. It was just the war.

I decided to believe that there was a reason for everything – there was something higher than me.

My imagination often started reminiscing of my days spent with the girl who I loved most – the girl who was now 150 kilometres away in the Serbian capital city of Belgrade, going to school and living a very different life. They had no war and didn't know what a dire situation Croatia was in. Daytime Serbian TV was all about dancing, singing and enjoying life. Meanwhile, Croatian national TV was full of misery, suffering and pain. It was no wonder, when the TV news was all about the war.

The beginning of December marked terrible news as Croatia had lost a lot of territory, a lot of land, villages and smaller cities. The fence was crumbling everywhere, but we had good leadership in the capital city, with experienced soldiers who had a strong allegiance to the cause and the desire to win.

When I look back, the enemy motivated us further as where they occupied territory, they destroyed everything. This raised our desire to defend our country and, one day, although we didn't know how or when, to liberate our country, our republic.

We had been forced back towards the capital cities and were developing fences around them. It was more reminiscent of First World War, with trenches dug around the edges of my city. Seriously, can you imagine digging trenches to defend a city in the twenty-first century? Osijek is the fourth largest city in the Republic of Croatia. Then it was a city abandoned by civilians was constantly bombarded for several months. You can't imagine how much rubble was on the streets, how many buildings had been destroyed and the sight of cars that had been left to rot. Women and children had gone a long time ago, which put even more strain on the soldiers. We established a static trench line around my unit, after which I was transferred to a fateful position by the last bus stop from my city, towards the village of Tenja at the old University of Agricultural Technology.

The university was a ghost town halfway between the city and the first enemy village in the middle of the fields. It was an incredibly exposed position. The side of the building was smashed from the ongoing bombardment and the windows didn't have any glass. We got used to walking our defensive line around the university, trying to keep out of sight. It was a huge building with so many rooms. We established our small quarters in the basement, strategically located in the centre of the building. The tall building could oversee all the fields around and the trenches on the right-hand side. The small artillery that we had was easily hidden between the buildings.

If the enemy was going to break through our lines, it was most likely that they would enter through the university. There would be nowhere to fall back to.

We couldn't simply just fight conventionally – we needed to fight their minds. Tactic-wise, the enemy needed to be continuously fed with information aimed at showing them that we would never fall back. This was a putting on a psychological brave face – helped by the local newspaper, which would report how many soldiers we had and all our new equipment. It was all a lie. We used to regularly change the insignia on our shoulders so, if any of the city's civilians were spies, they'd think there were lots of different units. The truth was there were always some new soldiers, but the only recruits were people aged fifty plus, who had been falsely mobilised or simply didn't have any other choice. I received a large number of soldiers of this type.

When there was no firing, it was quiet and silent. I used to walk through the university to the lecture rooms. I'd usually find lots of thesis books from professors, with handwritten notes and student assignments. I found myself wondering whether they had felt the war was coming. Would they ever come back to the amphitheatres and sit here listening to lectures?

The sound of broken glass followed my every step. I can still feel it even now, sending a chill up my body. It's such an eerie sound that came up from heavy army boots. You feel that the glass represents life and its cracking. Life is fragile, I tell my colleagues.

I started drinking. Some type of alcohol was always available. You found yourself having that glass of wine or beer or whatever pills you could find. You start with the pills – pills for headache, pills for colds. They numbed the pain because you were continuously cold and could feel pain in many forms. I don't remember how many times I felt every single fracture in my body, but the cold weather made them genuinely so painful. Then came much the stronger stuff, like cocaine. Cocaine was somehow available in the midst of everything going on. There was always somebody with cocaine and people were always having a hit. It was an unusual sensation – it just numbed all your feelings.

We talked about a lot of things and I struggled to listen to the older soldiers. They were at least ten years older than me, but I felt just as old in my body. In just a few short months, I had aged so much. I didn't pay attention because I didn't know whether I was going to live another day, another month or another year. All I knew was that this was the now, the job of being a professional in the armed forces.

All the older soldiers were typically worried about their kids and their wives. I could not relate to their feelings of not being with their kids, but I could understand them constantly thinking their wives were cheating on them. Most of these feelings were correct – they had been cheated on. They had been left and dumped. Their families had left to be refugees in other countries like Germany, Austria and Hungary. I was thankful to God that I didn't have the burden of worrying about my children or wife and what they were doing, where they were or even whether they were alive.

It is difficult to understand that you had a life a few weeks ago in your cosy house, and then suddenly you have to leave because you are afraid. So many of the people I'd met in my previous life were rough, tough guys. The moment the war started, when there were opportunities to take up arms and defend the fatherland, they ran away. Cowards, total cowards.

From time to time, I would judge others. Then I stopped being so judgemental and said to myself, "I could be somewhere else, but my parents didn't want me." Listening to all these stories was traumatic.

I was called into headquarters and spent five days in sniper school, training to be a line sniper, but not the kind who went behind enemy lines. There are two different snipers in the military – one a static sniper on the line, and one who goes behind enemy lines and carries out different types of killings or scouting observations. In those five days, I learnt a lot about how to be still, how to be calm, and how to accept life and death. Another pupil was a female surgeon. She was asking the finer points – where to shoot with the bullet, what to hit. *How easy it is to snatch a life from somebody*, I thought.

Funnily enough, a good friend of mine called Alex was learning next to me. I'd know him for many years. We had done a lot of beautiful things together, including going out and chasing girls. Now, here he was training with me to be a sniper.

We were allocated to be a pair and returned to the university. I would take a position in the far corner of a room and set up my 48 Karabin 7.9mm as high as possible. I would observe the enemy's movements and write reports. From time to time, we got the green light to shoot. The aim was just to disturb enemy soldiers who went past, regardless of their rank. It could be an infantry man, a tank member or an officer. Nobody cared – we knew we were helping save a lot of kids.

The scariest time was at night. On Christmas Eve, there were thirty of us at that university. You were surrounded by open space and the flat fields. I used to talk to the stars. It was so cold and the sky was perfectly clear. I was imagining being somewhere with a few girls, having drinks and enjoying ourselves. It's hard to comprehend what goes on inside your mind when you are on watch with one other person. You became a lone individual whose life was dependent on somebody else next to you. All we could talk about was the war or the girls – war, girls, war, girls – and what we wanted to do one day.

In the meantime, when Alex was sleeping, I would be at the observation post. Every time I saw a shooting star, I would make a wish to be happy, to survive the war and to be with my girl.

Sometime around 10pm that night I spoke with Alex and he said, "Do you see the snow moving?" We didn't have any night vision binoculars, so had to rely on our pure senses and the training we had done. I told him it was just snow.

Half an hour later Alex commented that the snow had come close to the edges of the university. I changed my position and looked out the window. I saw that the snow had been flattened by the weight of bodies. You could see the lines in the snow, like so many worms, giant worms coming towards us. The enemy had camouflage snow uniforms and they were crawling across the two kilometres of fields from the villages.

Just before midnight the shelling started. The enemy wanted to remind us that we would not be having a Christmas. There would be no drink next to the Christmas tree with the family – they were here. We were trying hard to cling on to our sense of determination. We all hoped the war would finish and we were going to be able to leave the city.

As soon as the shelling started, I told Alex I thought they had entered the building. We got on the radio to raise the alarm. Then we rushed downstairs and he started shooting. Maybe the guards had fallen asleep on the other side. As we were running down the stairs, the sound of cracking glass under our boots was so terrible.

Then everything stopped. Silence, deadly silence – and you're listening for where the next crack is going to come from. We were on level one and they were on the ground floor in a main corridor – near our quarters. I don't know where our other soldiers went. We were waiting for them. There was no synchronised defence. It was all about our survival. You simply have to defend your life, with no easy way of knowing who was on your side or the enemy's.

Suddenly, I heard that crack of glass. All my senses went so cold. We start throwing hand grenades. There were screams and shouting. It lasted for several minutes and eventually, we came to the quarters. The guard recognised me and yelled, "Lie down!"

They started shooting above our heads. We were crawling across that glass to reach our first guard, who was shooting from behind a concrete pole. Now at least we were with our troops. We started 'cleaning up' room by room, floor by floor, metre by metre, and it lasted until sunrise. In the morning, we saw bodies and traces of blood in the snow.

It was such a terrifying experience. As a kid I used to love the snow in winter, and now the snow had become my biggest fear. Everything is white or dark. There was no celebrating when we fought off the attacks – it was too terrifying an experience.

The fight for that place lasted a long time and there were several attempts to take the university. It had become a big obstacle for the enemy. Defending it was easier, given its solid concrete walls, big spaces and numerous rooms. It was also a great observing post and command centre. If the enemy had punctured that university, the entire line of trenches could be observed and access to roads controlled.

I remember I was sleeping on the first of January, but I don't remember being transferred into the static line from the university into the bunkers. All the soldiers were sitting there in the big shipping container that was dug deep down into the soil.

Most of soldiers in static lines were either younger than me or in their late fifties. Manpower was so low that mobilisation was called. No doubt the younger guys wanted to feel that thrill of war. I remember them coming in unshaved with long hair. They were cheerful and happy, but sooner than later I saw that the sparkle in their eyes disappearing. It reminded me of myself, six months before.

The guys spent most of time making the fires to keep everyone warm. Professional soldiers like me were always on lookout duty and filling sandbags. I had my M-53 heavy machine gun. It had powerful 7.9 millimetre calibre, which was almost equal those German models of MG42 and MG34 I used to man in previous months. The only difference was that this was the Yugoslavian version.

The frost was so strong that metal would stick to metal. I was ordering everybody to keep the weapons oiled and clean, and from time to time to shoot a few bullets just to make sure the metal would not stick.

The End of the War

"I lifted my head towards the sky and saw a beautiful golden orange line. A plane was flying up high and I told everybody very loudly, 'I'm going to be on that plane to Ibiza.'"

January 1992 saw something new. You felt something was coming in the air. We knew that the enemy could attack the city with all its armour, infantry and air power. There was real, continuous danger, but I truly believed that they'd chosen to lay low. There was no question they'd be able to storm the city at a later date, but we knew the winter was going to be formidable. Shooting would occur on the line and there would be a bombardment from time to time, but it was becoming less frequent.

Things were sort of coming back to normal life – whatever normal was. The thing is, it wasn't normal. What we didn't know, and what the politicians didn't share on TV, was that Croatia was going to be given independence by the European Economic Community.

I remember that day – 15 January 1992, sometime around 10 o'clock in the morning. I remember, because we had a phone meeting with the commanding officers. There was always some raised alarm or dangerous situation being explained to us, some potential attack. But this time, the point was that there was no attack coming.

The snow became white with the sun. It was cold, a few degrees below, but that sun on my skin was beautiful. We had got some new weapons, including some anti-tank missiles and rocket launchers. We felt like we were becoming the true army, not just a rag tag group. We still weren't uniformed like a proper army in peacetime – but we knew one thing: they were afraid of us. If they weren't afraid of us, they would have attacked us.

I believe the psychological warfare was playing a key role. The local radio station was always celebrating and making fun of the enemy with sarcasm and jokes. That kept us alive. They'd play certain songs to provoke the Serbians and Yugoslav Army. When the song *Lili Marlene* was playing, for example, shelling of the city was guaranteed! We used to call the radio station the 'Yellow Submarine', as sometimes when the shelling started we'd have to hide down in the basement – wet like a submarine – and listen to the radio there.

The End of the War

I was in the trenches and there was a TV in that basement. These soldiers were watching some foreign channel. Dear Lord, if only I knew how the fuck they found this channel on TV! At that very moment, I saw girls in bikinis dancing on the edge of the pool and jumping into the water. They had McDonalds burgers. I'd never seen McDonalds burgers before, never in my life. I'd heard of them, but never had the chance to try. McDonalds didn't come to Croatia until much later.

The beauty of everything I was watching sent me into daydreaming mode. Part of me was daydreaming, part of me was observing what was going on around me. For that moment, I was thinking, "Oh my God, I wish, someday."

The very next moment, I lifted my head towards the sky and saw a beautiful golden orange line. A plane was flying up high and I told everybody very loudly, "I'm going to be on that plane to Ibiza!" Everybody was laughing, smiling and making jokes. I laughed, too.

The others looked at me like, "You think you're going to be on a plane?"

I said, "If I survive this, yes."

Then the shelling and bombardment started again. I was thinking that this was like the First World War. I can't explain how many shells were falling on our city, on our lives. I was like, "Okay, this is it." This was the attack.

I saw the fear among the troops. You could cut the atmosphere with a knife. They were all breathing heavily. That bombardment was not normal. I had never felt a bombardment so intense, so constant and coming from every possible calibre of weapon. Rifles were shooting from the villages opposite. There were mortars, cannons, rocket launchers, missiles, everything. It lasted three hours.

We would only send people out of the bunkers to the observation posts for fifteen to thirty minutes, as they were much safer down below. Everyone was waiting for the enemy soldiers, and I was trying to preserve as many lives as possible.

Suddenly, at one o'clock, the President of the Republic of Croatia announced on the radio, "The Republic of Croatia is being internationally recognised. Independence is being declared for Croatia." So there were more countries, not just the Baltics and the Vatican, recognising us.

That was the reason the Serbs started shelling like it was their final push. I truly believe that if the shelling had lasted for another couple of hours, we would all be dead, severely wounded or crying for mercy.

We couldn't believe it when the shelling stopped. The U.N. said they would be sending forces into Croatia to support the independence. Somehow, I felt relief coming after seven or eight months of constant fighting. It was finally coming to an end.

Unbeknownst to us, there was a new war brewing in Bosnia and Herzegovina…

TO BE CONTINUED

Afterword

Looking back at my life from the safe distance of a forty-eight year-old, reflecting on what my life was like being thrown into the midst of a war, I can say that I consider myself extremely lucky. I was not smart, not skilled, not educated in survival techniques or leadership skills, but just purely lucky that I am still here. My luck was supported with countless dreams, and most importantly my everlasting quest for love.

I believe that we all have a destiny and a path in front of us. In my example, I know everything that happened to me had a purpose that I could not clearly see at the time.

Perhaps the point of life is to learn lessons. I did have a desire to be a soldier that was fuelled by watching too many Hollywood blockbusters and patriotic movies. I feel these led my subconscious mind to seek some of the brutality of war. Feeding a child's mind will result in the desire to be fulfilled in one way or another.

I could never have expected that war would become my life, nor that the only people fighting seemed to be lower and middle-class men, boys, sons and fathers. I was shocked when I realised how many big mouthed 'tough' guys would hide themselves behind their mother's skirts. I was amazed and fascinated by how cheap life is.

When you imagine witnessing a war, you often think of a battlefield, but it is much more than that. It is the destruction of homes, houses, and the lives of mothers who have lost their sons. It also reveals just how much alcohol can be absorbed by the human body, and how cheap propaganda can galvanise people.

With each day from July 1991, I found myself becoming older, more defiant of death, challenging God and the Universe – while simultaneously suffering in silence, knowing that if I died, my life would be for nothing. I would not have known what love was, or know the joys of having a family. With each day, I was turning into someone else – a man who wanted to preserve the life of other soldiers by training them as I had been trained. Leadership was not given – it was earned in combat. This previously naive nineteen year-old was getting more responsibility and accountability for the actions I was taking. The moment came when the boy had to stop being a boy and become a man.

The situation dictated it and you had to choose whether to become a leader or not. Leadership is about leading – creating that unbreakable bond between you, other soldiers and citizens who are staring at you with frightened eyes, believing that you are the one who will stop this madness of death, destruction and fear.

Even the strongest men have fears and can't prevent death. They have to accept life as it is, even when all you can hear is explosions from shelling by mortars, cannons and airplanes. You start thinking, *'If I am suffering all of this, then my enemy is enjoying it.'* You find yourself reaching into your darker mind and wanting to avenge all of those bad things being inflicted upon me, my people, my city. This spurs you on.

Fear is real. We all know how to talk when everything is rosy and beautiful – but in war, all that you have to control the fear is the belief that you know how to survive and protect your fellow soldier.

I had no idea of this before the war. I had a glorified view from *Rambo* and other movies. They don't show war as a challenge day after day, night after sleepless night, where the precious commodities were a shower, warm food and clean undies – all this while knowing the rest of world is enjoying freedom.

When the war first broke out, I didn't know who I was. I had no identity, and my entire family was broken. I felt betrayed by my government, my parents and my ex-girlfriend – all of them. Despite this, I am thankful. I learned to survive, I learnt to believe in myself and no one else.

I am thankful for those experiences – but I will never understand why others died and I survived. Perhaps it was God, or perhaps it was luck – who knows? All I do know is we were naive, young hooligans from the suburbs who believed that going to war was the right thing to do. It was a mistake. War doesn't need heroes – war needs flesh, blood and bones. As soon independence was declared and the U.N. entered Croatia, we were forgotten. Those who left become leaders, and I fought my way back. I found, though, that society only needs smart people, not warriors.

Today what I want to say to everyone that no one needs to be a hero. No-one needs to be successful to be happy. It is in all of us. If I, Mario the peasant, can do it, then everyone else can. That is the message of my book. Through suffering and pain, through bad decisions and choices, we grow. Time is the biggest commodity and no one has the money to buy time – so every second is important.

I am proud of being one among thousands of men who fought for freedom, democracy and independence. Communism was part of my life for many years and I didn't know what democracy was. I knew we had to do more than just stay quiet without standing up for ourselves.

The price for freedom is always high. It is paid for in life and in blood. No one can teach you how to live with true fear, the fear of dying. No one can tell you how to become a leader until you are given the choice either to lead or to follow, knowing that leadership brings with it responsibility, accountability and, most importantly, a duty of care for all around you.

This story may be full of uncertainty, full of horror stories and unhappiness – but in spite of that, there is always something there, something you should always believe exists – and that is hope. Trust me. One thing I can prove is that miracles *do* exist. All the tools you need to be happy, successful and loved are inside you, inside all of us.

I want others to draw energy from my book and use it as a survival guide, to help them progress toward success and realise that dreams really can come true.

– Mario

Index

A
Austria 10, 130

Austrian-Hungarian Monarchy 8

Axis Forces 43

B
Baptism 16, 44

Belgrade 104, 128

Bosnia 4, 26, 138

C
Catholic 16, 43, 44

Christmas 15-19, 83, 113, 131, 132

Church 9, 15-17, 43-44, 88, 124, 127

Communism 9-10, 12, 14, 23, 141

Croatian Police 30-36, 55

D
Democracy 9, 25, 40, 50, 56, 73, 84, 101, 121, 144

E
Eastern Block 8
European Economic Community 136
Ernestinovo 56-60, 88, 110

G
Germany 11, 23, 62, 130
God 10, 16, 44, 66, 68, 74, 104, 113, 127, 130, 137, 140

H
Herzegovina 4, 138
Hungary 8, 130

I
Ibiza 137
Independence 136
Italy 10, 43

J
Jesus 16, 124
Jews 10
Juvenile detention 5

K

Kalashnikov 34, 50

Kandit 12

Kumrovec 46

L

Laslovo 60, 69, 97, 111

Lenin 9

Lili Marlene 136

M

Marx and Engels 9

Mass 17

Matej 16-17

Mato 32, 39

Ministry of the Interior 46, 59, 73, 85

Mixed marriage 36

Molotov cocktail 48

Mortar fire 60, 69, 98, 102, 114-118, 137, 140

N

Nationalism 5, 9, 23, 44

Nustar 123

O

Orthodox 31

Osijek 8, 48, 128

Ottoman Empire 8

P

Papasha 39

Police 4, 9, 16, 30, 33, 36, 43, 47, 105

Priests 16, 43

Propaganda 105, 140

R

Rambo 47, 53, 55, 140

Religion 5, 25, 51

Romans 8

Roman Catholic 16, 43, 44

RPG 56, 98, 114

S

Secret Police 4, 9, 35, 43

Serbians 4, 23, 25, 27, 31, 36, 40, 56, 105, 128, 136

Socialism 10

Spagin 39

Special Forces 46, 48, 50, 56, 73, 89

Stalin 9

Stalingrad 62, 121

T

Tanks 34-36, 59-60, 69, 85, 88, 91, 102, 118-120, 122, 125

Tenja 128

U

University of Agricultural Technology 128

V

Vietnam War 47

Vinkovci 122

Vukovar 102, 121-124

W

WWI (written as First World War) 128, 137

WWII (written as Second World War) on pages 10, 39, 43, 59

Y

Yugoslavia 2, 5, 8-9, 13, 23, 25, 29, 30, 33, 50

Yugoslavian 4, 133

Yugoslav Federal Army 40

Yugoslav People's Army 23, 40, 45, 47-48, 71-73

Z

Zagreb 22

www.ingramcontent.com/pod-product-compliance
Lightning Source LLC
Chambersburg PA
CBHW071631080526
44588CB00010B/1367